LORD, DON'T LET IT RAIN AT LUNCH

More Devotions for Teachers

PATRICIA ANN FISHER

ZondervanPublishingHouse
Grand Rapids, Michigan

A Division of HarperCollins Publishers

Lord, Don't Let It Rain at Lunch
More Devotions for Teachers
Copyright © 1993 by Patricia Fisher
All rights reserved.

Published by Zondervan Publishing House
Grand Rapids, Michigan 49530

Library of Congress Cataloging-in-Publication Data

Fisher, Patricia Ann
    Lord, don't let it rain at lunch : more devotions for teachers /
Patricia Ann Fisher.
      p. cm.
    ISBN 0-310-60471-0 (pbk.)
    1. Teachers—Prayer-books and devotions—English. 2. Christian
life—1960– I. Title.
BV4596.T43F565 1993
242'.68—dc20   93–9893
                                                                    CIP

All Scripture quotations, unless otherwise indicated, are taken from the *Holy Bible, New International Version*®. NIV®. Copyright © 1973, 1978, 1984 by International Bible Society. Used by permission of Zondervan Publishing House. All rights reserved.

Edited by Mary McCormick
Cover design and illustration: Church Art Works

Printed in the United States of America

94 95 96 97 / DH / 5 4 3 2

Each one should use whatever gift he has
to serve others, faithfully administering God's grace
in its various forms.
1 Peter 4:10

I know God is real; otherwise, who opens
supermarket doors?
A first grader

For Kris
With love,
Mom

Acknowledgments

Special thanks go to my husband, Jim, and my daughter, Amanda, who have helped me every step of the way. I'd also like to thank all of those who have encouraged me on my journey, especially those teachers who wrote to me about *Lord, Don't Let It Rain At Recess*. I'd also like to thank Joyce Ondersma, Sandra VanderZicht, and Mary McCormick from Zondervan for both humor and great assistance.

Contents

About Prayer

I'm a believer in prayer. I can't teach without it. I pray about everything from how to reach a child to how to survive playground duty and rainy days. I pray all the time: for wisdom, for understanding, and always for enough courage to survive teaching first graders. The Bible gives us encouragement to pray—it tells us to "Pray without ceasing." That gives us fairly unlimited access and opportunity, it seems to me. It tells me that prayer should be more than a morning devotional, or a before-bed rendition of "Now I lay me down to sleep."

I think the Bible means what it says. Prayer is direct communication with God. THERE IS SOMEONE ON THE OTHER END OF THE LINE. We can talk to the Lord as we would talk to our best friend because that's who the Lord is! He's also the Lord of the Universe! (Talk about friends in high places!)

When things get difficult at school, I pray. When everything is going well, I also pray. I know that the Lord is waiting to hear from me. All I have to do is "call home." He's waiting on the other end of the line.

IN THE BEGINNING

*A*dams School quietly dozes in the searing heat of mid-August, the building starkly outlined by oppressive sunlight, its playground empty and still. Soft murmurs of awakening begin to echo through the halls as teachers arrive accompanied by armloads of summer collections for the school year. Gradually the building reluctantly abandons its siesta to the increasing sounds of a new school year.

I stand quietly in the hallway listening to the beginnings in the classroom of Kate, the second-grade teacher from across the hall. As I peer into her room, I see her tangling with a six-foot-long piece of paper that she intends to cover a bulletin board with, to brighten her room for her new class. "Hi, Kate," I smile. "Let me help." She nods in appreciation and the task is quickly completed. With two, it's easy.

"Now," she mutters as we stand back to admire our work, "if I could just find New Jersey." She moans as she sorts through a stack of names of states that, when put together, will represent the United States.

As Kate rejects each state, she piles them on a table. I carefully search through them. "You're right," I agree, "no New Jersey. I guess you could always teach forty-nine states this year and then tell the children that they'll learn about New Jersey in third grade."

She grumbles, "I'll keep looking. New Jersey was here last spring—I know it."

Continuing to visit down the hallway keeps me from getting to the task ahead in my own room. "Hi, Shelly," I call to the other first-grade teacher and my best friend on the faculty. "And how was the trip to Europe with Maggie?" Maggie, our third-grade teacher and a truly blithe spirit, had managed to convince Shelly to spend the summer in Europe with her.

"The best thing about the trip was that we were denied visas into Lebanon and Iraq," she sighs.

"But I thought it would be just the emerging former Eastern bloc countries and Scotland," I reply.

"That's what it was supposed to be," she cringes, "but then Maggie decided she could convince Saddam Hussein that peace is the best route, if she could only see him for five minutes. She even got an old military uniform from somewhere—you know, those camouflaged ones. Then she went to the nearest American embassy and kept announcing to anyone who would listen that "Great tasks are accomplished by ordinary people." She was so persuasive that I nearly went with her. Fortunately, the State Department didn't agree with her."

"Did you know," she continues tersely, "that we camped outdoors in Scotland without sleeping bags, just raincoats and umbrellas? Maggie thought it was the best way to catch the flavor of the place—the fragrance, the atmosphere. Frankly, I thought it the best way to catch pneumonia," she grumbles. "Well, I'm home now, and it's really a relief to be here."

"Maggie's a good, good person; everybody loves her," I comment, "but I don't guess you'll ever want to go on a trip with her again?"

"Well," she adds sheepishly, "I've never had such an

adventure-filled vacation. Who knows? I might just go with her again. Well, maybe . . ." She gets an amused glimmer in her eye and I realize that this vacation was just what Shelly needed! More power to Maggie!

Lord, thank you for watching over Shelly and Maggie and for the safe journeys of all the staff at Adams School. Be with us all as we begin this new journey, another school year. Amen.

MAY GOD BE GRACIOUS TO US AND BLESS US
(PSALM 67:1).

CAPTIVE!

*F*aculty in-service begins in the midst of the intense, searing heat of late August just when I'm beginning to feel butterflies of excitement in my stomach, curiosity about the list of names that will soon be my class, and enthusiasm for the new school year. For two days the teachers of Adams School will be held incommunicado while Peggy, our principal, reads the school handbook to us. The handbook that explains the school rules is also mailed to parents who apparently can read it for themselves. It's tragic that teachers can't read.

I reluctantly enter the conference room, resigned to squandering the day. Peggy has set out a tray with four dozen doughnuts and a pot of coffee. Since it's the beginning of school, no one will take a doughnut because we are all still on our summer diets. Later in the year we'll eat anything that doesn't move fast enough.

As I watch the rest of the faculty enter and greet each other, I cannot help but notice that everyone sits in the same chair he or she sat in last year, leaving limited choices for newcomers. It's a strange phenomena, and once everyone is settled in I long to shout from the old children's game, "Fruit Basket Upset!" which means: "Everyone find a new chair!" (Although if we had followed the exact rules, there would be one less chair each time we yelled. I'd volunteer to be the first one out!)

As the day drags on, so does Peggy's voice. The heat begins to penetrate the room, and I feel beads of perspiration collecting on my brow. There is air-conditioning in this room, but we can't use it because Peggy is concerned about "the misappropriation of public funds." In Peggy's view it has to be at least 100° outside to merit air conditioning. The mercury will invariably hover between 98° and 99° for the two in-service days. I wiggle and shift like a first grader, and it occurs to me that I'm becoming more and more like the children I teach, needing to move every few minutes. Shelly is sitting very still, but her eyes are closed. Olivia appears to be taking copious notes, but later I learn it is a letter to her daughter. Mary Ann is drawing a page of the cutest little mice.

But the eyes of the new teachers are glued to Peggy's every move.

I try to will the clock to move faster.

Peggy looks up. "Oh, by the way, you'll each have recess duty just one week a month. The kindergarten aides will also be on duty this year." Everyone looks dismayed—teachers begin each year clinging to the hope of escaping playground duty. Recess duty means teaching for four straight hours without a break of any kind, even a bathroom break. "You know," says Peggy, "recess duty is the most important thing we do. It enables us to really meet our children in a non-threatening environment."

All this time I thought I had met the children in a non-threatening environment in my classroom.

But then good old Maggie, our third-grade teacher, who has come to in-service for the first time in years says, "Then can we just do recess duty and leave?" We all begin to laugh, and even Peggy joins us (although I notice her laugh has little frowns around it.)

Lord, help me to focus on what is positive in teaching—the children, the other teachers, and sometimes even Peggy. No, Peggy's important too. There shouldn't be a "sometimes even" before her name. Amen.

ABOVE ALL, LOVE EACH OTHER DEEPLY
BECAUSE LOVE COVERS OVER A MULTITUDE OF
SINS (1 PETER 4:8).

THIRTY KIDS ARE ENOUGH

*I*t's lunchtime on the first day of school. Shelly is draped over two chairs, her back resting precariously against the wall of the teacher's lounge, absently munching an apple. I'm distractedly picking the watermelon out of my fruit salad.

"Bad morning?" I ask her.

"This is the worst class I've ever had," Shelly sighs. "I know I say that every year, but this really is the worst."

I nod in sympathy. "I wish I knew Japanese."

Shelly stares at me. "You have some Japanese kids this year?"

"No, I'm thinking of moving to Japan!" I mutter. "Or maybe an uninhabited desert island," I add tentatively.

"If you went there, it wouldn't be uninhabited," Shelly points out.

Marty, the kindergarten teacher, explodes through the door, "You two think you have worries. I had fifty-two kindergartners this morning. There were kids crying, hiding out under the tables, shoving each other, and throwing erasers. All over the classroom there were clusters of parents and younger siblings. At least four babies were trying to climb up my legs." She hesitates, to be certain that she has our rapt attention. She does. "Then there was this dog—a huge Doberman apparently totally attached to some kid named Sammy. Where Sammy goes so does Black Beauty. That's the dog's name: Black Beauty. Then Chris, the new kindergarten teacher got my aide because hers quit after the first ten minutes and Peggy thought that she needed an aide worse than I did. And to top it off I don't have a lunch because some child ate it," she finishes with huge sobs as she collapses at the table.

Shelly and I both rush to comfort her. "I'm so sorry, Marty, it sounds awful." As I pat her shoulder, her sobs wrench her whole body. I get a plate and divide my fruit salad while Shelly adds half of her sandwich.

"I'm not eating that," Marty protests as she shoves the plate away and rushes to the phone. "Yes, I want a large pizza with everything on it, extra cheese, a six-pack of Diet Pepsi, and a family-sized Caesar salad. And could you have it here in twenty minutes?" she asks.

Shelly and I exchange glances. Marty weighs about 110 pounds! Shelly begins, "There's no way you can teach fifty-two kindergartners."

"I know that," she says, grimacing, "but I had them all today." She takes a deep breath and sips the Diet Pepsi I have placed in front of her. "I've been told that the overload will go to Monroe School." She gets up, kicks the refrigerator door, and heads for the door.

"Where are you going?" I ask with concern.

"To get Sammy and Black Beauty transferred to Monroe," she asserts. "And to wait for my pizza," she adds resolutely.

"Any way you look at it," Shelly sighs, "thirty kids are enough."

I nod in agreement.

Lord, Marty is in need of your refuge today. Please let her know you are with her always even in the midst of fifty-two kindergartners. And help the

administration to understand that with five-year-olds—more is not better.
Bless and strengthen and sustain all of us at Adams School and all teachers
everywhere. Amen.

GOD IS OUR REFUGE AND STRENGTH, AN EVER-
PRESENT HELP IN TROUBLE (PSALM 46:1).

THE "W" WORD

I have a secret to tell you," I say conspiratorially to my class at the beginning of a burnished September day. First graders love secrets, so immediately there is quiet attention. Since moments of total silence are extremely rare in a first-grade classroom, I take a few seconds to enjoy this one before proceeding. "How many of you have heard about the W word?" They look at me with both startled and puzzled faces. Most first graders know there are certain letters of the alphabet that stand for words that are guaranteed to get them into trouble, but they haven't heard about W. They exchange glances, with little brows furrowed with deep thoughts. In a quiet voice, I confide in them. "This is the W word," I explain to them as I write *Wonderful* on the chalkboard. There is a collective sigh of relief as the children realize that I'm not going to talk about all the words they are not allowed to say. "It says 'wonderful,'" says Andrea, a dainty little girl who came to first grade, already reading.

"You're right," I smile at Andrea. "When you are wonderful, you are very special." I pause. "You are a *wonderful* class!" They grin and exchange knowing looks. From now on, *Wonderful* will be our operative word. "Wonderful," written on papers will be cherished. "Wonderful," spoken will be the highest praise.

But I don't know for certain that *Wonderful* has taken until Matthew retrieves his handwriting paper from my desk.

"What are you doing?" I ask gently.

"This isn't wonderful," he explains.

I look over the paper and nod. "You're right." It's not his best work.

"So I'm going to my desk to do it over and make it wonderful," he continues.

Expectation is what it's all about. Not just my expectation but that of the child about himself. It's contagious this *Wonderful* word. It's wonderful!

Our Father, who makes all things wonderful, help me to speak to the hearts of these children. Amen.

A WORD APTLY SPOKEN IS LIKE APPLES OF
GOLD IN SETTINGS OF SILVER (PROVERBS 25:11).

PLEASE DON'T CRY

*E*very fall at the beginning of school I'm prepared to have a couple of children who burst into tears when Mom or Dad leave them. It's always difficult to take care of the other thirty children when two are sobbing in the background. This year my crier is Katie. She meets all the requirements to be a crier. She's young, she's the oldest in the family (she's never seen a sibling go to school and come home again), and she hasn't been to kindergarten.

First I suggest to Mom, "Since she's so young and has never had kindergarten—" but her mother cuts me off at the pass.

"She'll do fine; she's ready for first grade. Maybe she'll do better with another teacher," her mom implores.

I say nothing knowing that if Shelly is her teacher the same process of adjustment will need to happen. Also, Shelly would never forgive me—she already has two children who are sobbers this year. "It will take some time to adjust," I tell her mom. "Just leave her and go about your tasks matter-of-factly. If you do, she'll come around. She needs to know that you feel secure about school and her ability to handle it."

But, of course, that's the problem. Katie's mom doesn't feel secure about leaving her child. She feels that she's abandoning her baby, and feelings are very contagious. I tell her that Katie is crying a little less each day, that the rest of the day is going well, but Katie's mom doesn't want to hear that. "Kids do things like this; she's just testing the water," I try to reassure her.

Eventually Katie does stop crying, but first grade is very difficult for her. I tell parents, "You probably could teach a child to roller-skate at three, but if you wait until six, she'll learn on her own." There is much to be said for readiness. There is much to be said about taking another year at the beginning when it is needed. But often pride gets in the way.

Lord, I ask your special blessing today on all the children who are having difficulty in adjusting to school. Grant wisdom both to teachers and parents. Also could you add a measure of patience for everyone who teaches? Amen.

LET YOUR CONVERSATION BE ALWAYS FULL OF
GRACE, SEASONED WITH SALT, SO THAT YOU
MAY KNOW HOW TO ANSWER EVERYONE
(COLOSSIANS 4:6).

THE GOOD OLD GIRLS

*C*lara taught second grade for fifty years before she retired. She was my father's first cousin in the days when family lived down the road. *Family* meant Sunday dinner, wading in the creek together, and helping with the harvesting. In Clara's home, *family* meant that the homestead belonged to her after everyone else had left or died. She kept the house the way it had always been, carefully cluttered with family memorabilia. In later years she added air-conditioning and a sun porch for luncheons with "the girls." "The girls" went everywhere together: to Chicago for plays and shopping at Marshall Fields, to visit relatives or other "girls," to church with Sunday dinner and a drive afterward. "The girls" were all young at a time when teaching was one of the few occupations considered appropriate for a woman. There was sometimes a lost love, a young man who had gone to France in the Great War and who had never come home. But even if this young man had been just a friend, or even a relative, his picture would still remain in a position of honor on top of the curio cabinet resting a lifetime on a hand-crocheted doily. There would also be another picture, row upon row of marching crosses marking the place that said that the young man would never come home again.

"The girls" kept the watch from the tragedies of war. They flew the flag from the front porch on every patriotic holiday. On

Memorial Day they stood on Main Street in red-white-and-blue hats and sold poppies to help "the boys" still in veteran's hospitals. Then they'd go to Clara's house for lemonade and conversation. "The girls" could talk and talk and talk; they'd talk for hours and hours with scarcely a breath between. There was no one that "the girls" didn't know even unto the fifth generation. They'd say to each other, "Well, you remember her? Her grandfather farmed out on the old Hinckley Road, and his father used to own the old James place out on the highway."

In the summer, "the girls" all went to summer school at the local teachers' college. "The girls" kept up to date on everything. Then they'd return to their classrooms and with infinite patience and perseverance would teach the youngsters reading and writing and arithmetic and everything else of value. If you were in one of "the girls'" classrooms, your penmanship was perfect and you grew up knowing where Belgium is. And you knew how to behave. Clara used to talk about a youngster who once said to her, "My grandfather is president of the college; I don't have to work."

And Clara responded, "Your grandfather sat at the very desk you're sitting at now." That was the end of that.

Retirement didn't even slow "the girls," as they still called themselves. They went everywhere, did everything worthwhile, and always had a wonderful time. Others started calling them "the good old girls," but it was spoken with respect and admiration.

Most of "the good old girls" have left us now. Sometimes I wonder if they're sitting on a back veranda in heaven, sipping lemonade. I know they won't have run out of topics to talk about. To the rest of us who teach, "the good old girls" left the a legacy of tenacity, dedication, patriotism, and morality. We could do no better than to become a "good old girl."

Lord, we thank you for "the girls" and the example they were to the rest of us. Help us to be the same kind of shining reflections of your love as they were. Amen.

THEREFORE, AS GOD'S CHOSEN PEOPLE, HOLY AND DEARLY LOVED, CLOTHE YOURSELVES WITH COMPASSION, KINDNESS, HUMILITY, GENTLENESS AND PATIENCE (COLOSSIANS 3:12).

THE TREASURE BOX

E ach fall I bring a lavishly wrapped large box to school. I
will have looked for weeks for just the right wrapping
paper and ribbon. The box has to look distinctive—after all, it is a
treasure box.

The contents of the box are ever changing. Everywhere I go
I find things to add to the treasure box. When I went to Hawaii, I
brought back shell necklaces (at five for a dollar they were a
bargain). From a convention I brought pins; there are books from
our book club, candy when it's on sale after holidays, and book-
club posters that I've laminated. Parents also get into the act.
Thang's mom stitches tiny heart necklaces. Maria's mom once even
made fudge—it didn't last long, though, because Kate, the second
grade teacher, saw her bring it, and the rest of the faculty staged a
raid.

To maintain the aura of secrecy, the treasure box is off
limits to everyone who has not earned a trip to it. Journeys to the
treasure box are earned with super-stars. And super-stars are given
for good conduct in the classroom like staying on task, completing
work, and good citizenship.

"Please, can't I just look into the treasure box?" Juan
Carlos asks mournfully one day. "Just a little look," he pleads, his
big brown eyes begging. "I won't even get close," he promises.

I shake my head.

"I have to get super-stars to get to look?" he asks longingly.

"Yes, but you can do it, Juan Carlos. I know it," I reply encouragingly.

Sure enough, the next week Juan Carlos earns a trip to the treasure box. As he sifts through the box, he grins happily. "There's so much good stuffs in here, Mrs. Fisher. But thems necklaces is the best. I'm getting one for my mom. But next week I'm getting one of those cars for me."

He's hooked. The treasure box has worked its charm.

Lord, I know so many of these little ones are going to have problems just staying in school. Enthusiasm and motivation are very contagious in the early grades, but later children can become immune. Help me to seize the moment and to make the most of each day. Amen.

HE WHO HEEDS DISCIPLINE SHOWS THE WAY
TO LIFE (PROVERBS 10:17).

BLACK BEAUTY AND SAMMY

*A*s it turns out, Marty gets both Black Beauty and Sammy. Sammy seems to be adjusting to kindergarten. Black Beauty is another matter. "Black Beauty always goes to the front of the line to reserve a place for Sammy. So Sammy is line leader every day," Marty complains. "After all, what five-year-old is going to argue with a Doberman? Or for that matter what kindergarten teacher is going to confront a Doberman?" she asks with exasperation. "Then when we have story time, Black Beauty comes to the circle and nudges his way to the front, and, of course, there's Sammy right along with him. Also, if there's anything Sammy wants, Black Beauty gets it for him. Yesterday Tommy Alvarez brought a huge set of crayons. All Sammy had to do was to give the dog a wistful look and Black Beauty calmly went to Tommy's table and grabbed the whole box in his teeth and deposited it in front of Sammy. Peggy is going to have to make a decision—either it's Black Beauty or me," she finishes.

Later in the day I see Marty with her class. Sammy is there, but I don't see Black Beauty. Still later when I go to the office, I notice that Peggy's door is open and there seems to be someone in there with her. As I take a closer look, I see Black Beauty lying contentedly by her desk.

"I see that you have Black Beauty keeping you company," I call to her.

"Oh, he's a lovely dog," she smiles. "He's happy just lying here all morning. Sammy's going to bring him in each morning and pick him up when he goes home. Black Beauty wouldn't hurt a flea," she smiles confidently. "He's just a very large dog, and he likes to display his teeth. He's just not ready for kindergarten."

I think Peggy's going to have far fewer discipline problems this year. Also, I'd better start praying that Black Beauty isn't going to be ready for first grade next year!

Lord, we never know when life is going to send us Dobermans. We do know your love will get us through it. Thank you, Lord, for the peace that knowledge brings. Amen.

IN HIS HEART A MAN PLANS HIS COURSE, BUT THE LORD DETERMINES HIS STEPS (PROVERBS 16:9).

MAY I GO ON?

*T*his class is one of the noisiest classes I've ever had. Every time we change subjects or retrieve books from desks, they like to visit and there is a delay in beginning again.

"You know," I tell them, "we just take too long to get ready. I'm going to start giving stars to boys and girls who can get ready without visiting." Now I'll have to make a mad dash around the classroom each time we start something new to award stars to the children who are ready. Teaching is certainly an aerobic exercise. I wonder how teachers ever teach from a fixed position in the room like a desk or a stool. Once I even knew a first-grade teacher who taught from a recliner. There were stacks of duplicated pages on her desk, and each time a child finished a paper, she put it on a nice little stack on the table beside the teacher's recliner. This teacher held a fly swatter in her hand and if a child deviated from the one-paper-after-another routine, she was called to the recliner for swats. I've always been grateful that I didn't get those children the next year!

My class is responding well to extra super-stars, but they still love to talk to one another. Sometimes I think I could just retire to the beanbag and they'd just sit and visit and visit. They aren't loud or boisterous; they just like to talk.

One day I decide that I've had enough. "From now on," I

tell them, "when we're ready to begin something I'll say, 'May I go on?' and you'll answer, 'Please do,' all together, because you are listening so well." They nod in agreement and we practice a few times. They like the bit about chanting "Please do."

From that time on, I'm not as nearly concerned about talking because anytime things get noisy, I ask quietly, "May I go on?" and they respond with "Please do." I'll add this to my basket of ideas. I still don't have a recliner, but on the other hand, I don't need to give swats either!

Lord, help me to be patient. These little ones are just six years old— help me to understand that always but still to expect the best from them. Amen.

BE COMPLETELY HUMBLE AND GENTLE; BE PATIENT, BEARING WITH ONE ANOTHER IN LOVE (EPHESIANS 4:2).

MAGGIE RIDES AGAIN

*M*aggie is dressed for roller-skating. She has on black tights, a purple mini-skirt, a ski sweater, a matching knit cap, and green neon roller blades. At least I think she's dressed for skating although this is also the outfit she wore for Back to School Night (minus the roller blades, of course). Maggie, our third-grade teacher, is having a terrific year at school. She arrived this fall in time for teacher's in-service. As usual, this year her classroom is cluttered with projects that remain obscure to the rest of the faculty. Library books litter the floor—the custodian hasn't spoken to her for years. Learning in Maggie's room is like an exclamation point—it happens during periods of intense excitement. There are many of those! Maggie remains somewhat of an enigma to the rest of us; we do know she's ageless because she's been sixty-two as long as anyone can remember. We know that she raised four children alone, yet she seems as full of life as any of the children in her classroom. The children in her class often seem breathless at the pace of learning. It's as if they are on an academic roller-coaster ride and enjoying every minute of it.

Today the third grade is off for Rollerworld for a day of skating. As we watch the third graders disappear into waiting cars at first recess, Shelly and I wave good-bye. "I guess she's going to skate," I comment. "I'd never have the nerve."

"Me either," Shelly agrees.

When the third grade returns at the end of the day, I can tell by the sounds in the hallway that something has happened. When the bell rings for dismissing school, I race to the door. "What happened?" I ask a group of third graders.

"Mrs. McDonald fell and hurt her arm—she's in the hospital," one of the third graders confides.

Alarmed, I ask, "When did it happen?"

"Right when we were ready to leave," a third grader moans. "She wanted to learn how to do a backward flip—like they do in gymnastics."

"Oh, no," I exclaim as I rush to tell Shelly.

Shelly quickly suggests that we go to the hospital. We lock our classrooms and tell Peggy that we are leaving to see how Maggie is doing.

When we reach the hospital, we see Maggie's doctor in the hallway. "How is Maggie?" I ask him anxiously.

"She'll be just fine," the doctor replies. "She has a broken arm; we're keeping her overnight because of her A-G-E." He spells the latter and looks around cautiously as he speaks as if expecting Maggie to assail him.

Shelly and I exchange knowing glances.

When we finally get to see Maggie, she is somewhat subdued. "I just can't figure out what I did wrong," she puzzles.

"You aren't going to try it again?" Shelly asks incredulously.

"Why not?" answers Maggie calmly. It's obvious that I did something wrong the first time!"

Lord, thank you for Maggie. Help her arm to heal quickly. And, if possible, Lord, help her ambition to be a gymnast on roller blades to be tempered—at least a little bit. Amen.

PRAY IN THE SPIRIT ON ALL OCCASIONS WITH ALL KINDS OF PRAYERS AND REQUESTS (EPHESIANS 6:18).

LOVE LETTERS

*I*f someone ever did a survey to ascertain who gets the most mail, teachers would win hands down. At the end of every day as I clean the top of my desk, I find my love letters. Most are folded into little tiny finger-smudged squares, but some are errant paper airplanes or have bits and pieces cut from them in an attempt to create a paper snowflake. In any case, at the end of the day, when I'm often the most tired or discouraged, I open my mail.

Andrea writes with her neat, careful script, "I luv u Misus Fisher." There's a note from solemn-faced Adam. "You my favrit teacher." There's a picture of a scribbled bouquet of purple flowers from Lisa. Juan Carlos merely writes the three letters he does know: d, r, and m. Sarah's letter is just a happy face like the one I often put on children's papers.

I've converted the wall behind my desk into a huge bulletin board on which I post mail. The children love to see their own letters and often point to them, glowing with pride. "I did that one," they proclaim proudly as though I'd never guess. After all, their names are on them!

Still, every day when I've said good-bye to the last of the strugglers and stragglers, I slip off my shoes, breathe a deep sigh of relief, and turn to my love letters. These scraps of paper are the best indicators of how I'm doing as a teacher. They let me know when I've reached a child; but still there are times when they leave me bewildered. Max, a wisp of a boy seemingly overwhelmed by first grade, writes the same note every day: "Dere Fisher." When I finally ask him about it, he shrugs. "It means Dere Fisher." And then he gives me a very large hug.

Lord, *sometimes there is so much to learn about these children that I'm certain that I'll never succeed, but each of them is too important for me to fail. Help me to keep the faith, no matter what. Amen.*

FOR IF THE WILLINGNESS IS THERE, THE GIFT IS
ACCEPTABLE ACCORDING TO WHAT ONE HAS,
NOT ACCORDING TO WHAT HE DOES NOT HAVE
(2 CORINTHIANS 8:12).

I KNOW WHERE I'M GOING

*F*or weeks I've been planning a field trip to a museum in the city about sixty miles away. It's to be a rather special trip to see a dinosaur exhibit. Afterward we'll have a picnic in a park. We'll go by private cars because there are no funds for school transportation this year. I've provided each parent with a map even though the directions are very clear: "Just stay on the highway until you see the Ellis Street turnoff. Turn right onto Ellis and go three blocks. You'll see the County Museum and a large parking lot where you can park for free." These are not even my directions— they came from the museum. No one should have problems with them.

As usual, we start in a caravan onto the highway, but soon other cars pass between us. I tell myself that no one can possibly get lost, but still I am feeling that something is not right.

It is not long before we arrive at the museum and after we park our cars we gather at the entrance. Everyone is here except for Max's dad, who is taking the day off work because he, too, loves dinosaurs. He was the only one of my drivers who did not want a map. "I know where I'm going," he insisted, but I gave him a map anyway. Now his car is the only one not here. The rest of us wait restlessly, the parents checking their watches surreptitiously. The children, too, are restless; they want to see what they came for. We continue to wait, watching for signs of Max's dad in every car that passes. I think of how often Max is lost in the classroom, and I'm starting to hope that it's not genetic.

Finally, a guide comes out of the museum. "Mrs. Fisher," she says, "If your class does not come in now, we won't be able to take you because we do have other classes coming. We'll watch for your lost parent and let him come in when he arrives."

It's the best I can do, so reluctantly I agree. Predictably, the children's voices echo with pleasure and glee, but all I can do is watch the door. With Max's father are Max, Juan Carlos, and David. Where are they? What if there's been an accident?

Max's father has still not arrived when it is time to leave the museum. I call back to school, to Max's house, where there's no answer, and finally to the police, who say, "Lady, call us again in twenty-four hours."

We go on to the picnic. It's a lovely, green oasis with plentiful play equipment, where hearing the children's voices would be sheer pleasure if I weren't so worried. "They're all right," Adam's mother tries to reassure me. "You know men drivers—they never stop for directions."

"I hope you're right," I say as she pats my shoulder comfortingly.

Soon we're headed back to school. Each mile of the way my fears intensify. These children are my responsibility. Whatever will I tell Juan Carlos's and David's parents? For that matter, what will I tell Max's mother?

But as we turn into the school parking lot someone shouts, "There they are!" Sure enough, there are Max's dad, David, Juan Carlos, and Max.

"What happened?" I demand as I jump from the car.

"Oh, we went off the wrong exit," Max's father comments cheerfully. "It was a one-way street, so I drove and drove and drove.

I just couldn't get off it. Finally I gave up and just took the kids to a movie. We had a ball!" Max, Juan Carlos, and David nod in assent.

I am not angry; I am furious. I'm also afraid that I can't say anything right now because I'd regret it later. As I walk away, Shelly comes up and puts her arm on mine and says, "At least they're safe. We were all very worried after you called."

Later I'll remember the field trip that Mary Ann took when she brought back an extra child, a terrified little Laotian boy who could not speak English—what a problem we had finding out where he belonged!

And later I'll think that with the number of field trips there are that it's a real tribute to teachers that so little does go wrong. At least I didn't explode at Max's dad. And one Saturday I'll take Max, David, and Juan Carlos to the museum.

Thank you, Lord, that I kept the peace with Max's dad. But please don't let him offer to drive for another field trip. Amen.

A GENTLE ANSWER TURNS AWAY WRATH, BUT A
HARSH WORD STIRS UP ANGER (PROVERBS 15:1).

CHEF FOR A DAY

*A*s Carrie approaches my desk, I note that she has a letter in her hand. "It's from my mom," she offers shyly.

I read it quickly at the same time that I'm collecting lunch money. Every year I have at least one mom who shares all the extraneous events in her life with me. It's evident that I'll not be disappointed in that regard this year!

> Dear Mrs. Fisher:
>
> Last night I was going to go to the grocery store when my friends Joe and Marie Hernandez came over. Maybe you've read about their son, Mark, in the newspaper. He's a terrific track star and even has broken some records that will live on in posterity. He's going to UCLA next year. I understand that they have an excellent track program there and who knows—he could be really famous some day. I always think it is good for parents to encourage their children in this way because it keeps them out of trouble. Carrie takes baton lessons now, and her brothers will play soccer when they are old enough. Carrie would also like to play soccer and if Fred, my husband, gets a raise this spring, we may be able to afford that. Joe and Marie used to live next door to us, but they built a new home out in Lavish Creek. I've always thought that the name "Lavish Creek"

is pretentious, but my husband, Fred, says that's because I'm an intellectual. I did always get better grades in school than he did.

We hadn't seen Joe and Marie since last Memorial Day when we had a picnic together at South Lawn Park. We rented a picnic area near the duck pond so the children could feed the ducks. My kids are never much for hot dogs, but when you have to feed a group there's nothing that will stretch so far. I love to make potato salad for picnics, but then you have to think of food poisoning, so I usually end up just bringing potato chips. I do know they have a lot of fat, so I don't permit them all the time, but I think that once in a while doesn't hurt. After all, it's one of life's little pleasures. When I say things like this to my husband, he always tells me I'm being philosophical again. I do like to read a lot. I'm reading a mystery right now that is very intriguing because even though no one in the book can solve the crime, I already know who did it! With so many kids it's gratifying to know I can still think. As I said, Carrie doesn't have a lunch today, so I've sent a few leftovers for you to microwave for her. I don't even have a microwave at home, but Joyce, my sister who lives in L.A., wouldn't be without hers for a minute. They lead such a fast-paced life down there. Rush! Rush! Rush! But even if I don't have a microwave, I do know you can't use foil in them, so I packed Carrie's lunch in plastic wrap. Thank you.
Carrie's mom

At lunchtime in the teacher's lounge, Shelly asks incredulously, "You aren't microwaving that for a student, are you?"

"I am," I reply. "Just don't ask any questions."

Heavenly Father, I need a dose of extra patience today. Also a longer lunch if I'm going to be the chief chef. Amen.

DISCRETION WILL PROTECT YOU, AND UNDERSTANDING WILL GUARD YOU (PROVERBS 2:11).

NOT A DAY OVER FIFTY

*K*athryn, a fourth-grade teacher at Adams school, epito-
mizes the professional teacher. Her methods are up-to-
date, her classroom well-organized, and her demeanor is calm and
gracious. She wears the latest fashion befitting a career teacher.
Even her roots are carefully dyed. Her slim figure is kept in shape
by jogging and workouts at a health club. I would never have
guessed that she was fifty, until Mary Ann had given her a birthday
party.

So when one day during lunchtime, Kathryn enters the
teacher's lounge, looking upset, she has everyone's attention.

"I just had an encounter with a parent," she begins.

We've all had those, so we nod sympathetically.

"It was awful," she shudders. "This woman—I don't even
know her—came up to me. She said that she thought it was
wonderful that I give so much time to the children and keep myself
in such good shape," she pauses.

We all exchange glances. It doesn't sound so bad.

"But then," Kathryn continues, "she said—she said—"
She stumbles. "She said that I look so good for my age. Then,
here's the difficult part . . ."

It *must really be difficult*, I think, because Kathryn's eyes brim
with tears.

"She said that I am just remarkable for a woman of seventy!"

We all gasp and make sympathetic sounds.

"She said it is just amazing that someone my age could still come to school every day. It was just awful," she finishes.

We try to comfort her with hugs, offers of coffee and Danish, but it's not comfort she's seeking.

"Do I look seventy?" she asks beseechingly.

"No," we echo in chorus.

"Some people are very strange," I offer. "You always look great, Kathryn. There's no way on earth that you look seventy. At all," I finish while everyone nods her assent.

But we all know that the words that have been spoken can really never be erased. Kathryn will remember them for a long time. In the next days I notice her fixing her hair self-consciously and even powdering her nose before recess duty.

It's absolutely fine to be seventy, but in our society, looking twenty years older than you are is an affront. How careless we can be with other people's feelings: How careless we can be with words!

Our Father, be with Kathryn in these difficult times. Help her to put aside those things she cannot change, to regain her confidence as a teacher and to ignore those who speak in foolish ways. Amen.

A WISE MAN'S HEART GUIDES HIS MOUTH, AND HIS LIPS PROMOTE INSTRUCTION (PROVERBS 16:23).

DITTO, DITTO

*B*ack in the good old days of education when a teacher had to make copies of anything, she had to use a mimeograph machine. When I first encountered these machines, they were all old and inevitably leaked large amounts of black ink. It was virtually impossible to use them without also giving your clothes and hands a dose of thick, oozing black stuff. (That is, if you were already competent to use them—which I wasn't!)

Teachers applauded the loudest when schools finally consigned the machines to the museum of mechanical monstrosities and adopted "ditto machines." These machines were not only faster but also dispensed less ink on nearby objects and people. Because the color of the ink was purple, many of the teachers of that era wore a lot of purple to blend in with the ink that did go astray. Even if a teacher did not reduce her wardrobe to purple, her clothes were often tinged with it, courtesy of the ditto.

When photocopiers hit the market, teachers became ardent and enthusiastic users. Finally, we had a way to make the copies we needed for classroom use without simultaneously destroying our wardrobes.

So this year when Peggy announced that she'd gotten out the old ditto machine, we all moaned. "The copier is to be used for office communication only," she announced at a teacher's meeting. "It's just too expensive for everyday use."

With color storming her face, Shelly had blurted, "I've never, ever used the copier for anything that I didn't need in my classroom. Isn't education the primary job at this place or is it office communication?"

Her words lay heavily on the total silence of the room. It was so quiet that a pin dropping would have sounded like an explosion.

The first disaster with the ditto machine came the very next day. Olivia, wearing a new blue patterned silk dress, got a liberal dose of purple ink on one of the sleeves. She said angrily, "This didn't have to happen. We can save all the money we need by eliminating administrators, all of them." (Peggy was not there to hear, fortunately.)

We go on because that's the thing teachers do best, but it's an uneasy truce, and open hostility is not far away. Then one day there is a note in our mailbox in the school office: "The ink dispenser to the ditto machine is missing. This part is obsolete, so until it is recovered the photocopier may be used on a temporary basis."

"All life is temporary," Maggie pronounces as she reads it and gleefully begins to use the copier. "And the part that is eternal hopefully won't be concerned with making copies," she adds.

At the next teacher's meeting I study the faces around me, certain that one of them is responsible for the missing ink dispenser. Shelly, Olivia, Kate, Marty, Maggie all look blissfully innocent. Probably I look the most guilty, but I KNOW that I didn't take it!

Heavenly Father, thank you for the moments when your tender mercy shines through clouds of discouragement. And thank you also for photocopiers. Amen.

GLADNESS AND JOY WILL OVERTAKE THEM,
AND SORROW AND SIGHING WILL FLEE AWAY
(ISAIAH 35:10).

THE CAKEWALK

*E*very class is going to have a booth at the Halloween carnival this year. Since the carnival replaces Halloween at school, I'm very grateful. All we have to do is find 100 cakes to give away! Adam's mother says, "You know, all the supermarkets have Halloween cakes. If we asked for the ones they couldn't sell by closing time, we could probably even get some donated. I'll be happy to be the supermarket mom."

We do get cakes from the supermarkets—dozens of them, and we don't even have to wait for closing to get them. We have also sent home a note to all the parents at school, asking for a donation of a cake. We get more cakes.

On the day of the carnival, voluminous numbers of cakes appear at the school. In fact, everywhere I look there are cakes: on every ledge and shelf in the storage room, on the table and counters in the office, and on the bookshelves, refrigerator, and microwave in the teacher's lounge. Just before school ends, I take my class on a field trip to visit the cakes. "Hands behind your backs—look only with your eyes," I implore them, knowing full well what could happen to these cakes with no encouragement at all. There are many wistful sighs, but the little hands stay off the cakes.

After school on Halloween, Adam's mom, Maria's dad, and I make a large circle on the school patio. Around the edge of the circle we tape laminated numbers. "Like a clock," says Maria who has stayed with her dad to help, "only more numbers," she finishes and does a cartwheel for emphasis.

At the carnival we sell tickets for ten cents. People line up on the numbers, and we start a music tape. For a brief minute, people walk from number to number, balancing carefully from one foot to the other. The music stops and Maria's dad pulls a random number from a gaily decorated box. The winner, flushed with excitement and pleasure, gets a cake.

All night we are very busy; our booth is by far the most popular. One woman says to me, "I don't even have children at this school. I just saw the carnival, and now I've won a cake!"

As the evening progresses, we become remiss about collecting tickets although we are certain that there is just one person per number. After all, I reason, this is supposed to be fun. Soon we no longer worry about any kind of rules.

We just play the music and give cakes away. Maria's dad yells to the crowd, "Don't leave without your cake," and Adam's mom and I just laugh and give out cakes. Juan Carlos and his sister each have a cake, the Garcia family has three (but they have nine children, so I give them another one.) Soon it seems that nearly everyone has at least one cake, and finally, to our immense relief, we are out of cakes! We've all captured the warm glow from the pleasure of giving. I might even do this again next Halloween!

Heavenly Father, the lesson of the cakes is one we all need to review frequently! It's not only better to give than to receive—it's more fun! Thank you for the instant joy we were able to witness in the hearts of some people who have little joy in their lives. Help us to cling to that joy. Amen.

DO NOT FORGET TO ENTERTAIN STRANGERS,
FOR BY SO DOING SOME PEOPLE HAVE ENTER-
TAINED ANGELS WITHOUT KNOWING IT
(HEBREWS 13:2).

THE DUNK TANK

*A*s I'm about to leave the Halloween carnival, I stop at the dunk tank. A huge tub has been filled with water and an intricate structure constructed above it so that when a ball hits the target, the person standing on the structure will get dunked. The person getting dunked is Peggy. It costs one dollar to dunk the principal, and the line to do it is very long.

"How many times has she been dunked?" I ask Liz, the school secretary who is collecting the money for the dunk tank.

"Fifty seven times," replies Liz with a worried look. It's a pleasant enough night, but still it is the end of October and definitely not swimming-suit weather.

"I guess it wouldn't do any good to say something to her," I comment.

"No, I learned that a long time ago. When Peggy wants to do something, she'll do it," she replies thoughtfully.

The next morning as I enter the office for my mail, Liz announces knowingly, "Peggy isn't here today. She injured her back getting dunked last night, and she also awoke this morning with a terrible cold."

By the next morning we're told that Peggy has pneumonia and will not be back to school for two weeks.

Liz shrugs, "Peggy always says, 'Life begins at forty!' But I think that might not be true when you factor in dunk tanks."

Lord, I ask your blessing and healing for Peggy. And also a dose of common sense. Just don't let her know I asked. Amen.

BECAUSE OF THE LORD'S GREAT LOVE WE ARE NOT CONSUMED, FOR HIS COMPASSIONS NEVER FAIL (LAMENTATIONS 3:22).

VETERANS' DAY

*V*eterans' Day is a day that often gets short shrift because of its location between Halloween and Thanksgiving. However, it gets special attention in my class because I think that learning about patriotism is important to the future. If we forget our history, we are in danger of losing our rights. I take every opportunity to encourage understanding of our country—Veterans' Day, Thanksgiving, Martin Luther King Day, Lincoln's and Washington's birthdays are all reasons for class units and celebrations. On Election Day we even visit a poll and one of the election officials will often show us a ballot. But this year I have a surprise for Veterans' Day. My son, Jamie, who served four years in the army has come to visit.

After his introduction, he asks, "What is Veterans' Day?" Several hands shoot up. Jamie points at Adam. "It's a day to honor everyone who fought for our country and helped defend it."

"Good going," Jamie grins. "Now there are three branches of service—the army and what else?"

Annie waves her hand furiously for attention. As Jamie nods to her she proudly answers, "The army, the navy, and the Salvation Army."

Jamie looks as if he might burst into laughter, but valiantly he goes on gently correcting her.

Meanwhile, Brenda's hand is waving, "Do women get to be in the army?"

Jamie nods, "Women do most of the things men do in the army."

Katie's hand is up. Jamie points to her. "Well, this is something I've always wondered about. What if a woman had to go to the army and she had to fight. Would she have to wear a skirt?"

Jamie looks a little nonplussed. "No, they wear uniforms just as the men do. It hasn't been decided for sure that women will fight in the ways men do. There're so many things that women are better at."

"What's all the jewelry you're wearing?" Anthony asks.

"Jewelry?" Jamie asks looking down at his uniform, puzzled.

"Yeah, all those pins and ribbons on your uniform," Annie adds.

"This is not jewelry," Jamie replies. "These are ribbons and medals for awards." He patiently begins to explain how he got each of them.

"I have all kinds of jewelry at home," comments Sarah.

Terri adds, "Me, too, and so does my mother; she's got four diamond rings."

Jamie looks desperate.

"Jamie, when you went to Germany when you were in the army, what did you do? Can you tell us about Germany?" It's Mom to the rescue.

Jamie gets the globe and carefully points out where Germany is and begins to explain what he did there.

After I dismiss the class for the day, he says, "How do you ever stand it—the Salvation Army, skirts, jewelry," he laughs, shaking his head.

"That was typical," I reply. "I once asked a class who the

vice-president was. One little boy said, 'Saddam Hussein,' and nearly everyone agreed! We had lots of work to do that year!"

Our Father, help me to teach not merely facts but to work for understanding in all things. Amen.

HOLD ON TO INSTRUCTION, DO NOT LET IT GO;
GUARD IT WELL, FOR IT IS YOUR LIFE (PROVERBS
4:13).

CHING CHINGS

*F*or several weeks now I've been hearing about a new Chinese restaurant in town. It's called Ching Chings, and everyone seems to be talking about it. It's the new "in" restaurant. When Jim, my husband, drops by school at lunch to share a stale sandwich, he says, "Let's give Ching Chings a try tonight." It takes me no more than a second to reply. I prefer nearly anything to my own cooking.

Later, as we pull up in front of Ching Chings, I notice a rather disconcerting sign. "It says, 'nonauthentic Chinese food.'"

"Maybe that's just a mistake," says Jim in an optimistic voice.

But as we enter the restaurant and my feet sink comfortably into a lush carpet and we are escorted to an immaculate-looking table overlooking a patio where hibiscus and bougainvillea bloom, I am reassured. As soon as we are seated, a waiter appears with a steaming pot of tea, and we slowly begin to relax.

"You'll never guess what happened today," I begin.

Jim shakes his head because he knows he'll never begin to guess the multitude of things that first graders can do or think.

At that moment we are interrupted by the waiter, "One, two, or three?" he asks briskly.

Startled, Jim says, "We haven't seen a menu yet."

"No menu," the waiter replies. Impatiently he asks again, "One, two, or three?"

"Uh, one, I guess," says Jim with bewilderment.

"Are you sure there's no menu?" I ask.

"No menu," he replies sternly.

"I'll have a one also," I reluctantly reply. It's beginning to sound a little like first grade in here.

We should not have been surprised when it took two waiters to unload various steaming dishes of food on our table. We should not have been surprised that the more we ate the more there seemed to be. Finally I said, "Well, I guess we know what 'nonauthentic' means."

Jim nodded. From years of eating my food he could tolerate nearly anything so when he pushed his plate away I knew the food was really bad.

"Not hungry?" the waiter asked as he removed the food. "What about dessert?"

We both brightened with expectation. Moments later the waiter solemnly set a mammoth platter of orange slices before us. We both stared in dismay at more orange slices than thirty first graders could eat. Suddenly we began to laugh and laugh.

We certainly didn't have a wonderful meal that night, but we did create a memory. Now when things get really difficult, we remind each other, "Well, we could go to Ching Chings for orange slices."

There is learning in all things.

Father, the memory of Ching Chings will bring us laughter long after we've forgotten the meal. Thank you for creating us with the ability to remember joys and laughter, to tuck away memories for a rainy day and then let them create rainbows. Amen.

AND DO NOT SET YOUR HEART ON WHAT YOU
WILL EAT OR DRINK; DO NOT WORRY ABOUT IT
(LUKE 12:29).

THE NOVEMBER VALENTINE

I'm just collapsing at my desk after school and kicking off my shoes when Carrie rushes back into the room, her lunch pail clanging against her side, her arms laden with papers, her jacket trailing behind her, her face flushed. "Oh, Mrs. Fisher," she gasps breathlessly. "I forgot Mom's letter and my valentines." She thrusts both at me as she hurries from the room.

Valentines, I wonder. *Valentines*. I sit back to enjoy the letter, smiling to myself.

Dear Mrs. Fisher:

I am sending this check to pay for Carrie's lunches on Tuesdays, Thursdays, and Fridays for August and September with the exception of Thursday, August 29, September 16, 18, and 24, October 16 and 17, October 21, and November 1, 2, and 4. Also is enclosed the money for the field trip to the museum. I've enclosed three dollars each for me, my husband, Carrie's two younger brothers, and my Great Aunt Edythe, who is visiting us from Minnesota. She came by plane. It was quite an adventure and that was why Carrie was absent last week; we'd gone to meet the plane. I do need you to send homework for that Thursday and Friday except for spelling that she'll work on next week.

71

Also, we've made the final plans for our vacation. Carrie will be gone February 8, 9, 10 and February 13, 14, and 15. So I am sending her valentines now. Please don't pass them out that day, but keep them for Valentine's Day. Also, please save Carrie's valentines. I know that some children just get valentines from discount stores and they don't amount to a hill of beans, but you know how children are. My husband's plant is retooling for two weeks, so we thought we might as well vacation then. We are going to Monterey to the aquarium and hopefully go on a whale watch. We're very active in Save the Whales. We're also very concerned about saving the redwoods. Since we're so close to the Sequoias I think we have to be leaders in protecting them even though the redwood that you can drive through is on the coast and not at all near us.

Thank you,

Carrie's mom

It's just November—how on earth am I going to keep these valentines until February without losing them?

Heavenly Father, every time I get a letter like this I think I'm not bright enough to be a teacher! I need wisdom, understanding, patience, and good humor—with a double scoop of the good humor! Amen.

A PATIENT MAN HAS GREAT UNDERSTANDING
(PROVERBS 14:29).

HOW TO COOK A TURKEY

We've spent the past two weeks learning about the Mayflower, Pilgrims, and Thanksgiving through art, drama, and music. Now it's Thanksgiving week and I've asked, "Who is going to have turkey for Thanksgiving?" Thirty-two sets of hands wave enthusiastically. "How do you cook a turkey?" I wonder aloud.

Susan's forehead wrinkles as she ponders the question. "Well, what I think is that you put it in the oven at about 28° for three hours. Then you make coleslaw and pumpkin pie." She quickly adds, "Fry hamburgers to eat." (What happens to the turkey?)

"I know how," Maria's voice bubbles with enthusiasm. "Put butter on the pan so the turkey doesn't stick. Put it in the oven for fifteen minutes at 50°. And then you get some stuff that's really good out of a can—I forget what you call it. Then save the turkey for Thanksgiving," she finishes.

"Yes, she's right," Andy nods, "only if you want it at Thanksgiving, you have to stuff it with rice. Then you put it back in the oven for one hour at 500°. Make more rice to serve with it," he finishes.

Linda adds, "A small turkey is best. You just bake it in the oven for ten minutes at 35°. Then you take it out of the oven and put garlic on it. A whole jar of garlic," she asserts. "Then you bake it again in the microwave for five to ten minutes. Take it out and let it soak for another five minutes." She shrugs her shoulders. "That's it," she adds.

"One thing I know," Adam says, smiling. "You have to take it out of the turkey paper. Then you put in the stuffing and stick those little metal things on the legs. Then take the turkey juice and mash it with beets and potatoes. Serve it with Jell-O, pumpkin pie, and a birthday cake."

"These turkeys certainly sound interesting," I comment.

Jennifer's hand waves wildly. "First of all you have to shoot the turkey. Then cut off the feathers and the head and legs—" She hesitates. "And anything else that sticks out. Then you put it in the pan at 19° for sixteen minutes."

"Mostly you just can't eat turkey," Juan Carlos observes. I guess listening to these recipes have given him just cause for this line of reasoning.

Mark agrees. "It's hard to cook a turkey. First you have to pluck it; then hang it upside down in a deep pit for one hour."

Sarah's hand waves for attention. "I know," she assures us, "that you have to put sliced lemons all over it. Then you cut it in slices and eat it. Be sure to say a prayer."

Amen to that!

Tomorrow we'll actually cook a turkey—as Linda says, "A small one is best" because first graders really don't like turkey much anyway even when their moms cook it. We'll have all the fixings, though, but no lemon slices or mashed beets!

Our heavenly Father, we thank you for all the blessings you have given us. Help us to be thankful always for what we have—a bountiful land, families, friends, schools, teachers, and even turkeys. Amen.

I WILL GIVE THANKS TO THE LORD BECAUSE OF
HIS RIGHTEOUSNESS AND WILL SING PRAISE
TO THE NAME OF THE LORD MOST HIGH
(PSALMS 7:17).

THE GREAT LAMINATING
DISASTER

W e needed a laminator at school because it would save
teachers a lot of repetitive work such as making new
letters for bulletin boards, saving priceless art, and the myriad of
other things that teachers think they need to keep. The school
district has one we can use, but the district office is four miles
north of never. And you have to have an appointment, which
means it can't be done at lunchtime or recess time or any other of
the chunks of time available to teachers at infrequent intervals.
Besides that, we could even afford one, thanks to our Halloween
festival.

The first laminator was cheap—just $29.95 as advertised
in a brochure. It consisted of a roll of laminating paper and a razor
blade. The instructions read, "Take care when using this machine."

"Machine," I gasped to Olivia, the sixth-grade teacher,
when I first saw it. "Machine," I repeated amazed. "Doesn't a
machine have moving parts?"

"I always thought so," she laughed. "Looks like we've been
hoodwinked." We both laughed and laughed. Soon Shelly came
into the office. "See our new laminating machine?" Olivia burst out
exploding with laughter. Shelly, being careful about opinions, lifted

an eyebrow and read the brochure, first looking astonished, and then seeing Olivia and me, she also began to laugh. The longer we laughed the less we could control the laughter and the louder we became.

Kate, the second-grade teacher, stuck her head inquiringly into the office. She stared at us for a full minute and then she, too, began to laugh. That sent the rest of us into even more hysterical laughter because Kate didn't even know what she was laughing about.

In the ensuing weeks Kate actually became quite proficient at using the "machine," but I didn't. By all accounts I'm the least mechanical person on the faculty and perhaps even in the town. In one attempt to conquer the machine I'd even managed to become so entangled in the laminating sticky paper that Olivia had to rescue me.

So it was with great enthusiasm that we gathered when a real laminator was purchased. The salesman began with, "There is no way you can use this machine incorrectly."

Everyone looked at me.

But this laminator was so easy to use that as days passed, I laminated and laminated, giving credence to another comment by the salesman, "When teachers first get a laminator, they laminate and laminate and even try to laminate each other."

One day as I was laminating away, I thought to myself, *This certainly is a breeze.* I wished that everyone would stop by and say, "Look at that; Pat is using a machine and is not breaking it."

Then, quite suddenly, the machine refused to work. There was still plenty of paper, but when I pushed "drive," nothing happened. I walked around the machine several times and even kicked its tires (it was on a cart), but it refused to work. I was standing there tentatively when the principal, Peggy comes in. "Problems?" she asks.

"It stopped working—I don't know why," I mumbled.

She carefully examines the machine. "Why you've laminated the machine to itself," she announces with shock.

But Peggy is good with mechanical things. So she fixed it.

Our heavenly Father, help me to learn the lesson of the laminator; we all aren't good with the same things. Help me to be patient with your little ones as they work to understand. Help me to always know that you can always "fix it." Amen.

PRIDE GOES BEFORE DESTRUCTION, A HAUGHTY SPIRIT BEFORE A FALL (PROVERBS 16:18).

SNIFFLES

*I*n November the rains begin, relentless rain in blinding streaks that lasts for days. Predictably, everyone turns up with colds, the teacher included. At this time every year I always get a sinus infection that spreads to my throat, and I lose my voice. A first-grade teacher without a voice is in serious trouble. As I collect my class that morning, I can barely croak a "good morning" to the children in line.

"Oh, no," they exclaim in sympathy. "Teacher lost her voice!"

During reading groups little noses are dripping all around the table. I can barely talk and my throat hurts. I reach over and put a box of tissues as a centerpiece for the reading table. I am reminded of a teacher I know who would collect money in the fall for tissues. If a child brought money, she would get her name on a list. The children whose names were on the list could use the tissues, but the others just sniffled away. There was no mercy or tissues for them.

By the end of the day I've sent three children home. Then it occurs to me that I'm sicker than anyone I sent home! I bring my lesson plans up to date, run off some extra material, and tell Peggy to get a substitute.

The next day I'm free to lounge by the fire, read a good

book, watch television, and drink spiced tea. The only problem is that I'm too sick to do any of those things!

Lord, I *seek your healing today both for me and for my first graders. Bring us back together soon. I miss them!* Amen.

BUT FOR YOU WHO REVERE MY NAME, THE SUN OF RIGHTEOUSNESS WILL RISE WITH HEALING IN ITS WINGS (MALACHI 4:2).

THE SUBSTITUTE

S ubstitutes come in all sizes, shapes, and ages. Most of the time they are competent and credentialed teachers. But sometimes when many teachers are out at once, the district runs out of able substitutes. I'm convinced that's what happened to my class.

The substitute arrived with a picnic basket and a knitting bag. She also arrived with a name that no one could pronounce, so she asked the children to call her "Mrs. Teacher." Jenny, the new kindergarten aide, was assigned in first grade because it was Mrs. Teacher's first day at our school.

It is Jenny who calls me after school. "Oh, Mrs. F, are you coming back tomorrow?" she asks anxiously.

"Yes, I plan to," I answer.

"Oh, that's a relief!" she sighs.

"Not a good day?" I ask her.

"When I went out to pick up the class, there was a unanimous and simultaneous groan. Wendy sighed deeply and said, 'Is Mrs. Fisher sick?' When I nodded, Maria moaned, and that set them all off. I did tell them that you would be back as soon as possible. That seemed to placate them for a while. Once they got into the classroom, they settled down right away just as they do for you."

"Well, you left very exacting lesson plans, right?" she goes on. "The problem was that she didn't follow them."

"Well, I guess that's all right if it was still a productive day for the children," I tell her.

"That is the problem . . . Oh, I tried, I really tried. It was just that she decided to change the room all around. First she changed seats and then she moved all the desks. Now all the desks face the window. And Juan Carlos is sitting in the hall. Then Mrs. Teacher had a huge hamper of food with her as if she were going on a picnic. All day she kept getting out the most delicious-looking, incredible snacks. My mouth watered all day."

"And the children are *always* hungry," I interrupt her.

"Yes, they looked at that hamper and looked at it. Finally, Juan Carlos just had to touch it. That's why he was sent to the hall. Then Philip cried and cried. Not soft sobs, more like loud wails. And so I had to take him out, too. Then Sarah got a headache and went home."

"It sounds awful," I mutter.

"You haven't heard the worst," she continues. "Mrs. Teacher gave out all the papers you had stacked in the corner, and then she knitted all afternoon—except when she was snacking."

I will be back tomorrow. I'm feeling better even though I still don't have a voice. But I will need to bring snacks for the whole class. After sitting for a whole day, watching someone eat mouth-watering treats, my first graders are going to be very, very hungry.

Lord, I think of all the classrooms I've seen with jars of peanut butter, crackers, oranges, apples, and all manner of food. Mrs. Teacher is definitely an exception. Thank you, Lord, for every teacher who cares enough to spend her own money for treats for children who never really get enough food. Thank you for every teacher who cares enough to make a difference. Amen.

JESUS SAID, "FEED MY SHEEP" (JOHN 21:17).

THE CONVENTION

*T*wo whole days off school and a trip to the coast. "I can't wait for the teacher's convention," exclaims Luci, one of our new teachers.

"I hope you have a great time," I tell her. "There are lots of interesting classes and exhibits."

After Luci leaves Shelly shrugs. "Who knows, maybe she will have a good time. I'm not going this year," she says emphatically. "I'm going to take two days of sick leave or even off payroll if necessary."

"I wish I could do that," I reply longingly.

"Well, why don't you? We'll go to the city instead. You feel just the way I do. They pack twelve of us and all of our suitcases into that old, smelly van at 3:30 in the afternoon. There is no air-conditioning or heat. They stop at 6:30 for dinner at this greasy spoon that Peggy loves. We finally get to the motel at 10:00 P.M., and to top it off, it's a motel I wouldn't leave my dogs at—old, funny smelling, cheap, and maybe even dangerous. Then there's one trip a day to the convention. We have to stay at the convention center all day without a place to rest even for a few minutes. There's no place to eat. Then we get back to the motel at 8:00 P.M. and go to another greasy spoon. Then we come back to the room.

There are three rooms for twelve of us. I'm tired of being treated this way. Teachers need to stand up for their own rights."

Olivia has come in while Shelly has been talking. "You're absolutely right, Shelly. We all work very hard, and this convention ought to be a treat instead of a miserable experience. You know, rooms at the Hilton aren't that expensive this time of year, and it's right next door to the convention center. We could all go in my car," she offers.

Shelly looks interested. "We'd have to pay for our own motel and other expenses, but it would be worth it to me."

"I'm in if Peggy says it's all right," I assent.

Peggy looks relieved when we ask her. "You'll be saving the school big bucks," she replies.

So Shelly, Olivia, Kate, and I go to the convention together. We ride in Olivia's new BMW. We wear our best clothes, go to classes and exhibits, and stop for lunch at the hotel. That evening we drive to the beach for lobster and sit by big windows overlooking the Pacific. The second evening we attend a production of *Annie* at a nearby dinner theater. And we talk and talk, first solving every problem each of us might ever encounter. Then we solve all the problems that education is ever likely to have. Lastly, we consider politics, world peace, and disarmament of nuclear weapons.

After the convention, Luci comes into my room. "I had to do the convention Peggy-style this year because I'm just starting to teach and money is a real problem, but I did want to tell you to reserve an extra room next year for Marty and me."

When Luci leaves, it occurs to me that Shelly, Olivia, Kate, and I are beginning to act like "good old girls." That's not a bad prospect. There is joy in life just waiting to be claimed.

Lord, thank you for the rest the convention brought to us. It seemed like a much-needed and long overdue vacation. Thank you for teaching and teachers and for the joy in all work. Amen.

THAT EVERY ONE MAY EAT AND DRINK, AND
FIND SATISFACTION IN ALL HIS TOIL—THIS IS
THE GIFT OF GOD (ECCLESIASTES 3:13).

I'M HUNGRY

*I*t's been a cold, wet day, and I'm eager to get home. The wind lashes violently at my rain slicker as I unlock the front door. Pulling the door closed, I sigh deeply as the warmth of the house surrounds me.

I hear the door close, and Amanda, my nine-year-old, comes barreling down the steps. "I'm hungry," she bleats.

I want to scream and stamp my feet, but that would take more energy than I have remaining. Instead, I open the door again and begin to walk down the steps with the wind and rain chasing me.

"Where are you going?" yells Amanda as she tugs open the door.

"Where no one says, 'I'm hungry,'" I reply, starting down the walk.

"Come back, Mom, come back. I won't say it anymore," she pleads.

It doesn't take much to entice me back into the warmth of the house. I hang up my slicker, kick off my shoes, and collapse on the sofa. Amanda slides carefully onto a chair, surveying me cautiously. "You didn't have a good day?" she inquires carefully.

I shake my head.

She slumps back into the chair, legs dangling over the arm.

Tomorrow I'll make a list of everything we have for snacks and post it on the refrigerator. On the bottom I'll write: "There are no caches of candy bars, ice cream, potato chips, or cookies anywhere in this house." I might even have it notarized!

Then I think of Amanda and how much I love her. "Amanda," I call. She bounces down the stairs. "Let's make cookies."

"All right!" she yells as she pumps her fist into the air.

Heavenly Father, sometimes the combination of the demands of family and job become overwhelming. Sometimes when I am so patient at school, I suddenly become impatient with the people I love the most. Help me to reserve a full measure of loving care for my family. Amen.

I CALL AS MY HEART GROWS FAINT; LEAD ME
TO THE ROCK THAT IS HIGHER THAN I (PSALM
61:2).

BEARING GIFTS

*A*manda and I are sitting on the floor beside a softly glowing fire, wrapping little gingham bears that we've made for my first graders. The fire casts a gentle light, and the fragrance of pine from our Christmas tree permeates the air as we listen to the carols of the season.

"They'll love these bears," announces Amanda as she finishes wrapping one and reaches for another.

We've already wrapped cellophane bags of goodies: oranges, tangerines, and candy canes. Tomorrow at our first-grade Christmas party there will be cupcakes, ice cream, and punch. For many of my first graders that will be Christmas for this year because the crops are poor and unemployment is high. I've worked very hard for these special moments with the children and already I've begun to anticipate them as we finish wrapping the last festive-looking teddy bear.

Saving time is a high priority for a mother of five. Therefore, I suggest to Amanda, "Let's put this stuff in the car trunk tonight. It will save time in the morning." But in the morning as I enter the garage, the car trunk is open and empty. I stare at it in disbelief. "Oh, no," I yell.

Jim, hearing my voice, runs down the stairs. "What happened?" he asks.

"The Christmas gifts are gone!" I exclaim in shocked disbelief.

"Look—the garage door has been forced," Jim replies, echoing my own surprise. "I guess you didn't lock the trunk?" he queries.

"No, I didn't." I choke.

"It probably wouldn't have made any difference," he tries to reassure me.

But that's no consolation for me. I finish getting ready for school, numb with shock. Who could have been so cruel to take the gifts of a first-grade class? Lord, what am I going to do? If only I had locked the trunk, if only I hadn't been in such a hurry, if only the gifts weren't gone!

At school the tree looks forlorn even with its festive attire. There are supposed to be presents beneath it today. What's more, I'd even told the children that there were going to be presents. *Lord, I need your help*, I pray with desperation. As I'm sitting at my desk thinking and praying, Adam's mom comes in. "I heard about the missing gifts," she comments softly. "What are you going to do?"

"Well, I have forty minutes at lunch; I guess I'll go Christmas shopping," I answer, but in my heart, I know I can't do it in forty minutes.

"I'll work on it this morning," she offers.

"Thank you," I mutter with some relief. At least there is one more person to share my grief with.

Reluctantly I get my class and begin teaching because I don't know what else to do. Small faces keep glancing at the tree and then at me. Finally, Max says, "You didn't forget Christmas presents, did you, Mrs. Fisher?"

"No, I didn't forget," I assure him. I don't tell him that my problems are much worse than that. *Lord, help me to think of something,* I beg.

Somehow time passes and as I take my class to recess,

Adam's mom calls to me from the office. "I've been calling stores," she says. "Stein's has those little stuffed bears that they were advertising for free when you bought $100 worth of merchandise. I thought perhaps they'd sell those to us, but they couldn't do that because of a promotion agreement. Here's the good news: They did donate thirty-two large bears about thirty inches each. They'll be gift-wrapped, and I'm going to pick them up at two," she pronounces with excitement.

"Wonderful!" I gasp in relief. *Thank you, Lord!*

"You haven't even heard it all," she continues with a huge grin on her face. "They also had those sample packages of food with oranges, apples, nuts, cheese, and a small ham. I guess they used them throughout their stores to encourage people to contribute to the city's food drive. Anyway," she pauses, "since it's so close to Christmas they're giving them to us, one set for each child!"

I look at her with amazement. "So I'll pick those up at the same time I get the bears," she finishes triumphantly. "It's solved."

"How will I ever thank you?" I ask.

"Well, you could be Adam's first-grade teacher," she teases.

After lunch I tell the children the story of the stolen bears. Momentarily their eyes glisten with tears of disappointment. "But this story has a happy ending," I reassure them. "The presents will be here soon."

They instantly resume their good humor and watch the door expectantly as we finish our work. Soon there is a loud shuffle in the hallway and Adam's mom, Joshua's mom, and Katie's mom come through the door, laden with gifts.

Soon there is absolute chaos amidst bears, ice cream, Christmas cookies, and punch. Happiness floats around the room on Christmas carols.

Later, Juan Carlos's mom will tell me how happy she was

for the Christmas ham to share with her family. "We had a real Christmas dinner," she says, smiling.

As I lock my classroom and drive home to share the blessings of the holidays with my family, I think about Christmas . . . cuddly bears, candy canes, the fragrance of pine, softly glowing candles. Christmas . . . a simple manger, a single shining star, three wise men, a troupe of shepherds, a choir of angels. Listen, you can hear them still. The Christ Child lives!

Lord, I'm overwhelmed by your love and mercy. Once again I am reminded that "we know that in all things God works for the good of those who love him, who have been called according to his purpose." Amen.

GIVE, AND IT WILL BE GIVEN TO YOU. A GOOD MEASURE, PRESSED DOWN, SHAKEN TOGETHER AND RUNNING OVER, WILL BE POURED INTO YOUR LAP (LUKE 6:38).

THE WORD BECAME FLESH AND MADE HIS DWELLING AMONG US (JOHN 1:14).

DEEP FREEZE

S helly and I share a common thermostat. It's supposed to keep the same temperature in both rooms, but in reality Shelly's room is always colder by 10°. The larger problem is that the thermostat sometimes doesn't work at all. To compound the problems, Shelly is always too cold and I am too hot. It sometimes strains the limits of friendship. Today is an icy winter day with a brisk chilling wind, but when I enter my classroom it seems nearly as cold as outdoors. The thermostat reads 42°. I turn the thermostat up, but there is no reassuring sound of heat coming on. I see Butch, our custodian, down at the end of the hall. I call out to him, "We have no heat." He quickly comes down the hall and, reaching into the room, turns up the thermostat. Nothing. By this time Shelly has already arrived and is still in her coat with a Scottish plaid scarf wound around her neck.

"The last time I was this cold I was out on the Scottish moors with Maggie," she shivers. "I can see it now, fingers of fog drifting over the moors and reaching out to chill the bone. I am not teaching without heat," she says resolutely as she heads for Peggy's office.

Soon Peggy is charging down the hall, followed by Shelly. "This is a minor problem," she mutters as she attacks the thermostat with a screwdriver.

I've retreated to my desk and am sitting down so I can pull my coat collar over my ears. Shelly is now also wrapped in a Scottish plaid shawl in addition to her coat.

"What are we going to do?" I ask Peggy. "The children are going to freeze. So many of them don't have adequate winter clothing."

"The teachers are also going to freeze," Shelly adds as her teeth chatter.

"You know, in Third World countries this would not be a problem," Peggy asserts.

Shelly and I exchange dismayed looks.

When the children come in, they exchange cries of "It's cold!" and settle into their seats. I've gotten some sweatshirts and sweaters from the school clothes exchange and for the first few minutes am occupied with distributing them. As I see them huddle in their seats, I tell them, "Simon says, 'Stand up!'" They grin.

"Simon says, 'Jump up and down ten times.'" They oblige.

Finally Adam raises his hand. "Could we just sit down, Mrs. Fisher? I'm so cold I'm jiggling like Jell-O."

At recess time Shelly and I make a huge tub of hot chocolate that we distribute to freezing first graders. We shudder and shiver through the rest of the day.

As soon as school is over, Shelly and I head for the teacher's lounge and hot coffee. "You know," I begin, "lots of teachers in Third World nations and probably some in our own country do have to teach like this every day, as Peggy contends."

"I know," Shelly sighs, "but we shouldn't have to. It doesn't help any of those people for us to be cold."

Butch pokes his head into the door. "Just wanted to tell you ladies that the repair guy said that the furnace is a load of junk. They don't even make the parts nowadays."

"I'm going home," Shelly mutters angrily as she gets up and storms away.

Soon I gather all my things together, too, and lock my classroom door, but as I head for the parking lot I notice a ladder leaning against the roof. I back up trying to see who is up there.

Oh, no. It is Peggy up on the roof. "Peggy," I yell, "you'll get hurt up there."

She walks tantalizingly near the edge of the roof and announces with careless disdain, "I am up here to fix the furnace." She waves a screwdriver for emphasis.

I decide that I can't leave without telling someone that the principal is on the roof. What if she were to fall off?

Reluctantly I head back into school. Liz, Peggy's secretary, is sitting serenely at her desk, her hands folded.

"Did you know that Peggy is on the roof?" I demand.

"Yes," she nods. "That's why I'm sitting here like this. I'm praying."

"Oh," I meekly reply. Certain of impending disaster, I have the sudden urge to run. I have to get out of there.

At home I turn the thermostat up to 80°, climb into bed fully clothed, turn the electric blanket up to nine, and call Domino's Pizza.

The next day both Shelly and I have heat although it is still 10° warmer in my room. I say to Peggy, "Did *you* fix it?"

She nods curtly, dismissing me. "Before there were parts you could order, there was invention. Necessity is the mother of invention."

Thank you, Lord, that we have heat again. And thank you that Peggy didn't fall off the roof. Please help her to ignore the inclination to solve every problem herself. Amen.

AND MY GOD WILL MEET ALL YOUR NEEDS ACCORDING TO HIS GLORIOUS RICHES IN CHRIST JESUS (PHILIPPIANS 4:19).

I KNOW THIS TERRIFIC BOOK

*O*ne of the most important tasks of a first-grade teacher is to teach reading. I believe that. I also believe that unless children learn to love reading that teaching them how to do it is very nearly irrelevant.

An intrinsic part of teaching the love of reading is reading to a class. Sometimes in the middle of doing something else I'll say, "I found this terrific book." Then I'll go to perch on the beanbag, and the class will huddle around me. They love to have me read to them. *John Patrick Norman McHennessy** and *Miss Rumphius*† are favorites this year. I could read either of these books all day and they'd sit and listen and still want me to read it again.

So one day when I see Max glance around cautiously and then slide out of his chair trying to hide behind the side of his desk, I watch him curiously, wondering what he's up to. Then he pulls *John Patrick Norman McHennessy—The Boy Who Was Always Late* out of his desk, and I see his finger begin to trace the words, his voice barely audible.

"Max, you'd be more comfortable on the beanbag with your book," I suggest.

---

*Burningham, John, *John Patrick Norman McHennessy—The Boy Who Was Always Late*. Trumpet Club: New York, 1987.

†Cooney, Barbara, *Miss Rumphius*. Trumpet Club: New York, 1982.

Flushed with pride for winning a trip to the beanbag, he strolls to the corner of the room, slowly enough so that everyone can see his triumph. "Could Juan Carlos read with me?" he asks.

"Of course," I answer, smiling.

Juan Carlos rushes to the beanbag, and soon there's a gleeful chorus of two little boys having hilarious fun learning to read.

It makes my heart sing!

Lord, thank you for moments like these—they make the moments of difficulty worth it! Amen.

I WILL SING TO THE LORD, FOR HE HAS BEEN GOOD TO ME (PSALM 13:6).

SPIRIT WEEK

*T*wo of the new faculty members, Marty, the kindergarten teacher, and Peggy want to have a Spirit Week at school during which everyone can demonstrate his or her loyalty toward Adams School and also have a little fun. I've not said a word against it because I know I'll be in the minority anyway. Shelly says, "Every time someone makes a comment about Spirit Week, you give an involuntary shudder."

"I do? I was just trying to play it cool."

She smiles. "It makes me angry, too. But both you and I feel learning is fun and that already is strange to most people."

"Spirit Week sends all the wrong messages. It says to the children that they need a break from learning because it's so boring."

But Spirit Week does come: On Monday everyone can wear roller skates at school. There are so many falls in my classroom that I begin to teach with my teeth clenched. I keep praying for the safety of all my little ones but also for my own sanity. In the midst of all the chaos I suddenly hear a crash near the beanbag, and as Juan Carlos looks up, all I see is blood all over his face. Oblivious to the rest of the class I rush him to the office where Carol, the school nurse, and I try to discover where all the blood is coming from. By mopping his face with gauze we eventually can see that it's a cut on his chin. "It will take some stitches," Carol announces. "I'll just take off to the emergency room with him. I know his parents have no phone, and we do have a permission card for him to receive emergency medical care."

The sound of Juan Carlos's piercing screams echo throughout the school as Carol takes him out of the office. I watch her trying to reassure him as I return to my own classroom. It's very quiet when I enter; there is almost a hush in the air.

"Everyone take off your roller skates now," I announce crisply. There is a chorus of disappointment, but these children have come to know that there are times when I can't be budged and that this is one of those times.

On Tuesday everyone wore hats. Maria and Jose wore Mexican sombreros that were at least six feet in diameter. On Wednesday the children wore school shirts if their parents could afford them. Thursday was backward day. Jean zippers do not open in the back for very practical reasons. On Friday it was free-for-all day, which meant "anything goes."

I know that I do not ever want to do a Spirit Week again unless it's preceded by Holy.

Lord, these children need every second I can give them. I know that. Help me to use my moments productively even at times like this. Lord, help me not to complain so much about small things that I won't be heard about things that count. Amen.

DISCRETION WILL PROTECT YOU, AND UNDER-
STANDING WILL GUARD YOU (PROVERBS 2:11).

FINDERS, KEEPERS

I have a hard time finding things. I'd like to be able to say that this is merely a sign of impending age, but I can't do that because I've always been rather absent-minded. I know where the important people in my life are, such as my family and my class, but I can never find a pencil.

Every year my class seems to learn rather rapidly that although their teacher can teach, it's their job to find the chalk.

I've tried to reform and become more organized, but it's not in my nature. For a while I'll think, "Remember, the star stamp is by the vase in the middle of the desk!" I try mentally repeating the words: *star stamp, star stamp*. But then I get out the pretend money for an auction for math. "Listen up," I tell the class. "This is a real auction for posters, bubble blowers, and all kinds of really wonderful things! The first hand I see with forty-seven cents gets a choice! Come one, come all," I invite. "The auction is about to begin!"

Sarah's hand waves wildly and as she proudly displays a quarter, two dimes, and two pennies, she chooses the kitten poster that she's admired for a long time.

"Who will give me thirty-eight cents for this marvelous neon-pink car? It's guaranteed to win every race—well, maybe some at least."

Joshua is the first to wave his money in his hand, his big blue eyes full of pleasure. As he holds his treasure in his hand, he stops for a second to admire his purchase and to wave triumphantly to the rest of the class.

"What about this balloon?" I ask. "Notice how huge it is, and it's made of the very best balloon materials." For emphasis, I give the balloon a good tug. "Just eighteen cents for this lovely balloon."

Joseph's hand is up, and I'm so pleased that he's on task that I tell him, "You also get a super-star." For a moment I look at the vase thinking, *star stamp, star stamp,* but it isn't there.

Sarah says, "It's in your hand, Mrs. Fisher." And it is indeed. I quickly give Joseph a star, and then there's another for Sarah and finally for the whole class because they are all so eager and enthusiastic. Then I carefully put the star stamp by the vase although I know that the next time I look for it, it won't be there.

Help me, O Lord, not to lose a single one of these little ones of yours and to always know the difference in importance between people and things. It would, however, be wonderful to be able to find some of my things occasionally. Thank you that I always have so many people around to help me! Amen.

ASK AND IT WILL BE GIVEN TO YOU; SEEK AND YOU WILL FIND; KNOCK AND THE DOOR WILL BE OPENED TO YOU (LUKE 11:9).

CHICKEN POX

Dear Mrs. Fisher:

I'm writing to tell you that the spots on Carrie are not chicken pox. Her brothers do have chicken pox, which they got from their cousins, Tony, Alisa, and Mark, who do not go to this school because they live in Los Angeles. Their mother, Joyce, is my sister. She is two years older than I am but her children are the same ages as mine. Carrie's birthday is August 19 and her cousin, Tony, was born on June 5. George (Carrie's one brother), was born July 7, and Alisa was born December 23 (it's always hard for her at Christmas time because she doesn't get separate gifts from people). Although I do remember birthday gifts for her, my brother Tom and his wife, Joan, and their children who are ten and twelve don't ever send any. Their children are named Courtney and Cassie, which are nice enough names and I sort of like it when all the names in a family can start with the same letter and sometimes I wish I had done it with my own children but there you have it—it's done as it is and I'll just have to live with it. Mark (my sister's youngest) has a birthday on January 10 and Carrie's youngest brother, Eric, has a birthday in November, which is bad news because I know the school and they'll probably want to keep him back a year, which may cause problems with teasing from Sean, his older brother.

Oh, by the way, Aunt Edythe did go back to Detroit. She really liked the trip to the museum and said that

you are certainly a good teacher even though you're no
spring chicken.

Thank you!

Carrie's mom

After I read the letter, I sent Carrie to the office where,
Carol, our school nurse (I don't know her birthday) sent her home
with chicken pox but not before she exposed the whole class to
infection.

Dear Lord, I need a dose of patience (badly) (and soon). Amen.

LOVE NEVER FAILS (1 CORINTHIANS 13:8).

THE BEANBAG

*I*n a corner of my room I have a bookshelf lined with first-grade favorite books and beside that a beanbag for collapsing. The beanbag is for rewards—like finishing work. It's also for someone who is having a bad day. Sometimes it's for someone with a headache. Sometimes it's for someone who stayed up late last night. Sometimes it's used for someone who is "tired of working." Sometimes even other teachers send in a member of their class for an r-and-r.

Whatever the justification, the beanbag is a priority in first grade. Getting to go to the beanbag is a triumph. Children will often greet their parents after school with "I got to sit on the beanbag today!"

Parents sometimes come in to look at the beanbag. "So this is the beanbag," they'll comment, looking totally puzzled that it's just an old blue plastic beanbag. Sometimes parents even buy their child a beanbag for at home, but they discover it's not the same.

The beanbag at school is a first-grade treasure. It can't be transplanted. Imagine, for example, the Jefferson Memorial in Burbank! While Burbank is a very lovely city, the Jefferson Memorial simply does not belong there. Likewise, the first-grade beanbag cannot be moved to a new place. Second and third graders often come in and say, "Oh, I remember the beanbag," and their eyes become distant with nostalgia and longing. The beanbag is a place of peace. It's an integral part of my philosophy of education.

Lord, we all need beanbags in our lives, places of refuge and comfort along the way. Help me to understand that always with my first graders, other teachers, parents, and my own family. Thank you for being our ultimate refuge and salvation. Amen.

HE WILL COVER YOU WITH HIS FEATHERS, AND UNDER HIS WINGS YOU WILL FIND REFUGE (PSALM 91:4).

DELIVER ME FROM RECESS DUTY

*I*t's been a cold day with strong winds galloping across the playground. On this windy day I have recess duty and I feel bone-chilled. Besides, windy days do something to children—it's as if the movement in the air is contagious. On windy days I've always thought that it would be appropriate to attach strings to the children and let them fly like kites. At least then I'd have control of the strings!

It's also been a day of hearing "Tea–cher," pronounced with two elongated syllables, "He hit me." Or "Tea–cher, she won't play with me." I'm not in a mood to be a peacemaker. I need a break from all of this. Do I really need this to understand the children in my classroom? Am I that obtuse? It distresses me to feel that recess duty is so inexplicably tied to a teacher's job that most principals see recess duty as a kind of test: If you can't do recess duty, then you're not fit to teach children.

Olivia, near retirement, confided to me yesterday, "I may have to retire early. Every time I have recess duty I can barely make it through the week. My old bones can't take it—I need that break." Because Olivia has a different recess and lunchtime from me this year, I haven't seen her very much, but I have gone into her room and the spark and sizzle of learning is in the air. Reaching and teaching sixth graders is a task of courage and commitment. Olivia has both. We need teachers like her—we need her wisdom, her creativity, her knowledge, her understanding.

If I were a principal, I'd say, "Olivia, I'll do just about anything to keep you around. Whatever it takes."

Instead, Olivia's quiet resignation will be accepted in the spring. We'll have a tea for her (even though she doesn't drink tea), give her a corsage (even though she's allergic to flowers), and point her firmly toward the nearest pasture. With her will go thirty years of teaching expertise, a master's degree in math, and a love of all things academic.

If Olivia were a statesman, she'd just be coming into her prime. But she's a teacher, and it's all over.

Lord, I know that Olivia has so much to give to all of us at Adams School. She's needed here. Age seems a senseless means of measurement—Olivia is so young in spirit. Lord, I feel helpless and discouraged and it's difficult to find the words to pray . . . Amen.

HEAR MY PRAYER, O LORD; LET MY CRY FOR
HELP COME TO YOU (PSALM: 102:1).

A FUNGUS AMONG US

I am awakened early with the sound of rain skipping on the roof and tapping at the windows. I am not fully awake, so I try to convince myself that it's Saturday, that there is no impending alarm. When suddenly the alarm does go off, it sounds like a mad dog preparing for an attack. Quickly I get up to turn it off, and then I push the vertical blind aside to look at the rain. It falls with a steady, calm intensity that indicates that this is not a frivolous, impulsive storm but one that has come to stay. Reluctantly I head for the shower.

At school the other teachers are tight-lipped and grim. Peggy is flying a new rain flag, a black banner with scarlet letters proclaiming: "RAIN." It does not contribute to good humor to see the haughty flag flapping breezily in the wind and rain. "It might as well be a skull and crossbones," Shelly comments sharply. "I sometimes think the flag makes it look as if we have a plague." I'm not feeling even that cheerful, so I just nod in agreement.

The children are happy to come in out of the rain and quickly get ready to work. Everyone earns a super-star. I try to match their contagious enthusiasm, and soon we're busily at work on the morning's tasks.

At recess time I permit the children to get a snack from their lunches if they have one. Most of them eat the federally funded lunch at school, so snacks aren't abundant. I have carrot sticks, oranges, and peanut butter and crackers at school, so I quickly prepare snacks for the children who don't have one. Juan Carlos makes it all worthwhile when he gobbles his snack hungrily and says, "You sure are a good cook, Mrs. Fisher."

We play Simon Says for a couple of rounds. Then I take the children to dart for the restrooms, and I watch them splash merrily through the puddles. There is nothing quite as wonderful as having restrooms outside, an architectural phenomenon of California.

The room takes on a good-humored buzz as we settle back to work. After a while it's time for lunch. The school cafeteria is being used this year to house two classrooms of children we didn't expect, so we line up at the cafeteria window to take lunch trays back to the classroom. Peggy's flag continues to wave mockingly in the breeze. Back in the classroom, Andy promptly drops his tray. Naturally it's mashed potatoes and some kind of meat gravy. I send him back for another tray while I work on cleaning up this mess.

Maria says, "You never get mad when someone drops a tray, Mrs. Fisher."

A long time ago I learned that not getting angry saves a lot of grief and emotion. Besides, I'm the mother of five and I've seen worse. Many, many times.

In the afternoon we write a story and work on an art project for our Arctic Animals unit in science. At the last minute I decide that we'll do an extra art project, and soon everyone is cutting out penguins. Still, the afternoon is long without recess. My stomach grumbles because I've eaten only orange slices. I'm tired, and a headache is creeping up my shoulders. I need a break. I have a new book at home that I think of with longing. Finally, as it's time to go home, Liz, our school secretary comes in with a note: "There will be an emergency staff meeting after school." I moan silently.

Fifteen minutes later there is no humor in the staff room. As everyone sits down to await Peggy, it's very nearly silent. As she comes in she announces, "There's a fungus among us." Everyone stares at her.

One of the new teachers gasps, "Is it contagious?"

"Where's Olivia?" Peggy asks. We shrug. No one knows.

"About this fungus among us. I want it stopped," Peggy snaps.

Shelly whispers, "What on earth is she talking about?" I can't even hazard a guess.

Peggy proceeds, "This fungus among us is causing real problems."

"Like what?" asks Marty looking totally befuddled.

"Those of you who are involved know very well what I'm talking about."

"Just think about it," Peggy storms as she strides out of the room.

We are still sitting in shocked silence when Olivia arrives barely managing an unwieldy six-foot-long sub sandwich. "I thought the meeting would last forever," she explains. "At least this time I thought we wouldn't starve, too."

Olivia cuts the sandwich, and, as we all sit munching hungrily, Shelly comments, "What would we ever do without you, Olivia? There was also a hunger among us."

Later Shelly and I discuss the "fungus." "About all I can think of is that some people are not getting along together," I suggest.

"Have you noticed any problems?" she asks.

I shake my head. "It's just very strange."

We never found out what the fungus among us was, however. It remained one of the illusive things a school administrator does.

Dear Lord, as a teacher I know it is better to focus on that which is positive. It's also impossible to solve a problem that hasn't even been defined. If there is a fungus among us, please cure it, Lord. I ask your continuing blessing upon the whole staff. And, Lord, I pray, don't let it rain at lunch tomorrow. Amen.

BE DEVOTED TO ONE ANOTHER IN BROTHERLY LOVE (ROMANS 12:10).

SARAH'S BABY

Sarah is a darling little first grader. Her raven hair is always neatly pulled into a pony tail that hangs as a thick braid nearly to her waist and is always banded with a colorful bow coordinating with her outfit of the day. Susan, Sarah's mother, works very hard. I know, because she is the fifth-grade teacher at our school. Sarah's father, Joe, goes to the nearby university to become an engineer.

Susan longs for another child. "I love Sarah so much," she confides to me. Joe will finish university studies in June and already has a job. I want another baby and so does Joe," she finishes. "We've been on the adoption list for four years. Four whole years," she moans.

Sarah says longingly, "We have a nursery for a baby at our house. It's all yellow, and when you walk into it, it's like sunshine smiling."

Then Michelle's mom has a baby, then Max's mom. Sarah says forlornly, "I think it's our turn."

The months begin to pass. Carrie's mom has a baby. Susan's eyes look so sad. "I pray and pray and pray," she says.

"There will be an answer, Susan; we're all praying for you, too," I reassure her.

It's after school one early spring afternoon blessed with

warm sunshine when Liz comes into my room. "Have you seen Susan?" Then as she sees Susan, she says, "Oh, Susan, I thought you might be here. You're supposed to call your social worker."

Susan looks at her with sudden understanding and as she races out the door she yells, "Pray for me."

Together Liz and I go to Shelly's room after collecting Maggie, Marty, and Olivia on the way. Maggie launches into prayer at breakneck speed and the rest of us bow our heads in unison. No one, no one interrupts Maggie when she prays. Maggie is just catching her second wind when Susan appears in the doorway.

"It's a girl," she squeals. "Born yesterday, can you believe!"

Immediately we all surround her with hugs and questions. Thank you, Lord!

The next day Sarah can't wait to share her news. "We got a baby," she announces proudly. "Her name is Caitlin, and she has hair and fingers and toes."

Juan Carlos says derisively, "All babies got them stuffs."

That's not nearly enough to slow Sarah down a second. Every day we hear a little more about the new baby.

One day I say to Sarah, "How's Caitlin? Does she talk yet?"

She appraises me thoughtfully. "No, she doesn't talk yet, but she does purr. She purrs and purrs and purrs!"

Heavenly Father, we thank you for the gift of little Caitlin and for her whole family. Bless and keep them in your love and care. Amen.

LET US HOLD UNSWERVINGLY TO THE HOPE WE PROFESS, FOR HE WHO PROMISED IS FAITHFUL (HEBREWS 10:23).

THE CATHEDRAL

*A*dam has finished his work for the morning. He's been to the back of the room, where he collected blocks, Legos, and unifix cubes in every hue and size. Back at his desk he intently begins to assemble them, totally absorbed in his task. Joshua stops at Adam's desk and asks, "Can I help?"

Adam shakes his head, unwilling to be distracted. His small brow is crinkled in concentration. Joshua shrugs and looks at me for support. I shake my head. Clearly, Adam does not want to be interrupted.

As more children complete their work, there is a growing buzz of activity. Still Adam works on as an intricate building begins to emerge.

"We need to clean up for lunch," I announce. While the rest of the children scurry to get ready, Adam clearly doesn't even seem to hear me.

"Adam—lunch," urges Joshua in a loud whisper.

Adam looks around as the rest of the class sits quietly, hands folded. "Mrs. Fisher, is there any way I can work on this at lunch? I'm building a cathedral."

Not eating lunch with the faculty is a small price to pay for a cathedral, I decide.

"Maybe we should pull your desk into a corner so you

won't be interrupted," I suggest during lunch break. He nods in agreement as we carefully manipulate his desk into a corner without disturbing his workmanship.

"My dad has a book on cathedrals at home," he explains to me as he briefly nibbles a sandwich.

After lunch I read a story, we write in journals, and then we write a story together. Adam is still building a cathedral.

Later that afternoon as we're getting ready to go home, Adam puts the finishing touches on his project. As he stands back with pride, we look at his cathedral with admiration. It's so intricately constructed that it seems an impossible task for a first grader.

Later, as I think about the day, I realize that I spent the day teaching first grade, but Adam—a mere sprite of a boy, freckle-faced with wire glasses resting uncertainly on his nose—Adam was accomplishing great things! Sometimes the best way to help a child is to get out of the way!

Lord, it seems to me that most of teaching is getting out of the way. A teacher is a guide who shows the pathways and encourages the travelers. Help me to be a good cheerleader for these little ones. Amen.

AND WHAT DOES THE LORD REQUIRE OF YOU?
TO ACT JUSTLY AND TO LOVE MERCY AND TO
WALK HUMBLY WITH YOUR GOD (MICAH 6:8).

TOOTHLESS ANNIE

*F*or a first grader there are few more exciting moments than losing a tooth. There is high drama in the classroom when there's a loose tooth. It's like an Academy Award for six-year-olds. Today it is Annie who has her first loose tooth. I hear about it this morning when I go to the playground where all the children are lined up.

"Teacher, teacher," yells Kathy. "Annie has a loose tooth!"

Annie gets out of line to run up to me. "See," she points to her open mouth. A tooth is dangling by a slender thread. "It wiggles and everything and sometimes there is even blood," she reports somewhat gleefully.

"You could just lift it out," I suggest. "It's ready."

"Oh, no," remonstrates Annie with all the feeling of a Sarah Bernhardt.

All day I hear about the tooth. Annie tells me, "I'm not feeling well enough to do math; my tooth hurts."

And later, "Do you have a Band-Aid?"

"Band-Aids don't work for loose teeth," I explain, my patience wavering.

"Maybe I should have an aspirin," she suggests. "Maybe I should lie down on the office cot for a while," she adds.

"I think you'll be fine, Annie," I answer, "but you can sit on the beanbag until recess; that's ten minutes." This time the beanbag reward is for me. As Annie plumps up the beanbag and settles into it, I know I'll have ten minutes of peace.

But I have recess duty this week and there is Annie on the playground, surrounded by a gaggle of first graders. She has a long length of paper towel jammed into her mouth. She's certainly playing this role to the hilt.

It's mid-afternoon as we're starting to clean up for the day when Annie comes running to my desk. "My tooth, my tooth came out," she yells triumphantly as she holds up the tooth. "But I'm bleeding!" she moans.

"You'll be fine," I assure her. "Go to the restroom and rinse out your mouth. Here's an envelope for the tooth."

Soon she returns and says, "Where's my sticker?" As I hand it to her, she sticks it carefully on the tooth chart that is meant to keep track of such momentous occasions.

"Oh, look at that, will you!" exclaims Juan Carlos. "I can hardly wait to lose a tooth!"

Not much on the achievement scale beats losing a tooth. Even second and third graders, some of whom I don't even know, beat a path to my door for a tooth sticker and for that very special recognition that comes from losing a tooth.

Heavenly Father, little Annie really taxed my patience today. I ask a special blessing upon this little girl. She's a dear, sweet little one when she isn't losing a tooth! Thank you for her life. Strengthen my patience, perseverance, and love—especially for Annie but also for all my first graders. Amen.

IF ANYONE SERVES, HE SHOULD DO IT WITH
THE STRENGTH GOD PROVIDES, SO THAT IN
ALL THINGS GOD MAY BE PRAISED THROUGH
JESUS CHRIST (1 PETER 4:11).

THE LOST SHOES

When can we go roller-skating like the third graders?" asks Jacob one morning.

I think to myself "Never!" but in an effort to be more charitable I reply, "I'll have to think about that." Translated that means: "Maybe you'll forget all about it."

But a few days later Jacob again asks, "Did you think about going roller-skating?"

Seeing his hopeful look, I reply, "We'd have to work very hard to do that—like reading five hundred books. But that wouldn't really be work—it would be fun," I smile.

"Yes," the class replies in unison, exchanging excited grins.

"Well, I tell you what. I'll make a bulletin board that will help us count books. When we read 500 books the very next Friday afternoon, we'll go roller-skating." I don't tell them that I'm not doing a backflip like Mrs. McDonald did. In fact, I don't even tell them I'm not going to skate. Having one faculty person in the hospital after roller-skating is quite enough for one school year.

My class accepts my challenge, and every day they have extra time to read. What a rewarding time this is for me! Maria has collapsed on the beanbag, deeply immersed in a book. Katie and Sarah are propped on elbows on the floor, reading *Brown Bear*.

Annie sits at her desk, twirling a strand of hair and carefully sounding out words. Max has found a pillow to lie on and a corner to read in. A flower-scented spring breeze stirs the air. Except for the mumble of reading, the class is quiet and peaceful. What a blessing it is to me to see them contentedly reading like this. It's even worth a trip to Rollerworld. Deciding to contribute to the cause, I take out a book of my own to read.

The day we reach 500 books, I take the class to the playground and teach them a cheer: "Someone in the crowd yells *yeah* for first grade, someone in the crowd yells *yeah* for first grade. One, two, three, four, who you going to yell for? First grade, that's who." Over and over we cheer.

"You're wonderful," I assure them, but they already know that.

Six moms offer to drive and help put skates on, and five of them will also skate. As I watch the children start to skate, I see some of them tentatively clutching the rail, carefully lifting the skates, one skate then the other, tongue tucked in teeth, foreheads crinkled in deep concentration. Others skate full speed ahead interrupted only by falls at frequent intervals. A few have done it all before and wave at me breezily each time they pass.

This has not been as bad as I remember. As the skating session ends, I ask the moms to be certain that everyone leaves the skates and takes shoes.

I am back at school with my group first. School is just dismissing for the day as the children come in to get papers and lunch pails. Just as the last first grader leaves, Marty, the kindergarten teacher, comes in saying, "I found Juan Carlos crying in the hall."

Juan Carlos throws his arms around me, his little body shaking with sobs. "What is it, Juan Carlos?" I ask.

"My shoes, my shoes," he sobs.

Sure enough, he is just stocking-footed.

"You left them at Rollerworld?" I ask.

He shakes his head, "No, I got my shoes," he explains. "They just don't fit no more," he sighs as he holds them up.

I hug him. "We'll get your shoes. It's just a mixup—someone else took them by mistake." I head for the school yard, but most of the first graders have already gone.

I take him to the school clothes closet where donated clothes are left. "We'll just borrow some shoes, and I'll call each boy in the class, and we'll find your shoes." Just what I wanted—a day at Rollerworld followed by a night on the phone.

But Juan Carlos shakes his head and cries even louder.

A pig-tailed little girl whom I recognize as Juan Carlos's sister peeks into the office. "C'mon, Juan Carlos, we have to go home."

"We have a problem," I tell her. "Juan Carlos and another child must have gotten their shoes mixed up at Rollerworld. The ones he has are too small."

"Oh, Juan Carlos," she shakes his shoulder. "Those are your shoes. My mom said they were too small this morning; she could barely get them on. She's going to get him new ones when the check comes today. C'mon." She nudges him and jerks his shoes on his reluctant feet.

"Brothers," she mutters to me as they leave.

"First graders," I mutter to myself as I return to my room and sink into my beanbag, totally exhausted.

Lord, today I was reminded once more that no matter how long I teach there are new things to be learned! Please help me to learn these things with grace, tact, and a bit more energy! Amen.

NEVER BE LACKING IN ZEAL, BUT KEEP YOUR SPIRITUAL FERVOR, SERVING THE LORD (ROMANS 12:11).

THE SECRET MISSION

*I*t's a beautiful spring-kissed day. The cherry tree across the street waves its blossoms in the breeze. The lilac bush by the office has burst forth the fragrant blooms. The house down the street has a row of marching tulips. Above, the sky is bright blue with fluffy white clouds. It's too beautiful a day to spend indoors.

When I go out to pick up my lunch line, I tell them, "What we're going to do now is very secret." They nod listening with anticipation. "The rules for this secret mission are that you have to be in a straight line and you have to follow the person ahead of you with no talking at all. It's like 'follow the leader.'" They agree, anticipation glistening in their eyes.

"And one last thing: You have to look all around," I add. They're ready.

I begin to lead them around the school, past the lilac bush, across the street to the cherry tree, by a robin busy with her nest, and down past the marching tulips. The next yard has bright-pink roses climbing over a trellis.

They are very quiet. We look like a mother duck and her ducklings out for a walk. I haven't said a single word, and they are also very still. There's almost a hush over the class.

Soon we turn around, going back over the same path.

Passing drivers look at us, puzzled, as we wind our way back to school and to our classroom.

"We went for a walk," Juan Carlos yells as we enter the room. Not talking has been a strain for him.

"What did you see on the walk?" I ask.

"Flowers, all kinds," says Sarah.

"There were even roses," adds Annie.

"And those purple flowers—lilacs, I think," adds Justin.

"What about the sky?" I ask.

"Oh, it has all kinds of poofy clouds," Adam comments. Katy says, "It's a very pretty blue."

"And people looked at us," smiles Martin. "They never knew that we were on a secret mission."

"We'll never tell!" I add conspiratorially. They shake their heads. "What season of the year is it?"

"Spring," they chorus.

"We're going to write stories about spring on this very special pink paper," I tell them as I pass out the paper. "It's Pink Day—we have pink paper and something else pink—pink lemonade!" As I bring out the container of lemonade, the room is filled with oohs and ahs. "When you start your story and I see you working, I'll bring you your glass of pink lemonade," I finish.

At once they go to work. No one spills the lemonade. A happy buzz settles over the class. Soon there are hands raised all over the room with stories and pictures of flowers to share. Except for Max, who just writes, "Dere Fisher."

Lord, thank you for the world ablaze with the beauty of spring. The trees and flowers shout of your glory and the birds sing of your love. All praise be to your holy name. Amen.

THE HEAVENS ARE YOURS, AND YOURS ALSO
THE EARTH; YOU FOUNDED THE WORLD AND
ALL THAT IS IN IT (PSALM 89:11).

NO SAD SONGS

*M*aggie is distributing lovely floral invitations today for a dinner party for Olivia. "No spouses, no kids, no administrators," they state unequivocally. I'll have to think twice about going to Maggie's house. For one thing, she has a German shepherd, a huge creature who greets guests so effusively that they invariably bounce to the floor. Second, Maggie has never thrown away a single thing in her whole life, and, what's more, she's never put anything away either. This results in every chair, every table, and every corner being littered with papers, boxes, and everything else that Maggie thinks she could need some day. Guests at Maggie's house not only cannot find a chair to sit in; they're lucky if they can find a piece of floor to stand on. Still, even with all of these disadvantages I know that I will go because the party is for Olivia.

On the night of the party, Maggie is not there when we arrive. Her German shepherd stands guard at a screen door and growls menacingly at us.

"This is the right night?" Shelly asks worriedly.

The rest of us nod. Maggie's house is on a very busy street, and we all feel strange loitering around the front yard.

"Here she comes," I yell as Maggie's car comes roaring into the driveway with Maggie waving wildly. Behind her screeches a catering van driven by an anxious-looking young man. "Follow me," she motions to us as she leads us past the house into the backyard. There she has set up tables on her brick patio. Each table is decorated with crisp pink linens and centered with bouquets of fresh pink roses and candles. Tiki torches give the patio a warm glow in the dusk and cast warm shadows on Maggie's immaculately groomed garden and pool. "Maggie, it's beautiful; you've worked so hard!" I comment, and the others agree with soft murmurs of delight.

Maggie's eyes glow mischievously. "You didn't think the old girl had it in her, did you?" she grins. As the caterer quickly sets up a lovely buffet of fresh fruits, pastas, salads, and baked ham, Maggie energetically produces delicious hors d'oeuvres from the caterer's tray.

We are soon all talking, laughing, and thoroughly enjoying Maggie's wonderful dinner. "There's dessert, too," Maggie announces when we've all eaten and eaten and eaten. "By special order, the caterer baked our desserts without calories," she jokes as varieties of fresh fruit tarts, cheesecakes, and chocolate mousse are placed on the buffet table. "But before we indulge," she says, "I'm going to tell you a story. A long time ago my husband up and left me with four kids. I just had a high school education, and the only job I could find was waitressing. Believe me, these were tough times. I knew I had to go back to school, and I knew it would have to be at night. A friend offered to watch my kids and she did—four nights a week for four years with no pay at all." She stops, in teacher style, to be certain that we're all aboard. We are. "We'd all love to have a friend like that, wouldn't we?" Our heads nod, but our eyes are slowly turning to a blushing Olivia. "This friend," she continues, laying her hand on Olivia's shoulders, "says she's retiring. Imagine retiring, and she hasn't even seen sixty. Let me tell you now, I'm doing her recess duty for the next ten years. If I can crawl and climb all over the Scottish Moors and learn to do a backflip at Rollerworld, I can do an extra recess duty. Well, Olivia, dear, it's your turn to talk," she finishes. We all begin to clap.

Olivia stands up quietly, blushing darkly. "I don't know what to say," she gropes.

"What about 'I accept'?" prompts Maggie.

"I accept," Olivia says quietly. "Thank you, dear friend," she says to Maggie, hugging her. We all start mopping tears.

"Stop sniffling," Maggie commands. "There should be no tears when there's dessert to be eaten. And also no more talk about retirement."

Amen, Amen, Amen!

BUT SOMEONE WILL SAY, "YOU HAVE FAITH; I HAVE DEEDS." SHOW ME YOUR FAITH WITHOUT DEEDS, AND I WILL SHOW YOU MY FAITH BY WHAT I DO (JAMES 2:18).

REMEMBER PEARL HARBOR?

Dear Mrs. Fisher:

I am very concerned about Carrie. We did know that she was very young when she came to school. Her younger brother will be coming to school next year. He's not at all like Carrie. He likes to read books and has since he was two. He's so excited about coming to school. His name is George. He's named after his great uncle George who is married to Great Aunt Edythe. Great Uncle George didn't come with Aunt Edythe when she came to visit us. He was an aviator in World War II, stationed in Pearl Harbor on that infamous day of December 7, 1941. That day he had off, so he wasn't hurt in the attack, but our family is very proud of him as you can well imagine. (Oh, by the way, our youngest son, Mark, is just like Carrie. I was hoping that he'd be more like George but he isn't.) But back to Carrie's problem. She just can't seem to stay on the subject. When she starts to talk she has to include all the details surrounding the subject and just never can get to the point. It can go on and on and on and sometimes it really upsets me so much that I just want to yell to her, "Get to the point, get to the point." My husband, Fred, whom you've never met because he works the night shift, says it must run in the family, and to be truthful, his family is a bit loony tunes. In my family we don't have that. My sister is at Georgetown University in law school and both of my brothers are graduates of UCLA and my other sister is a clerk at K-Mart. I think she'll do better when the kids are all in school. It's very hard for a mother to work and to have to worry about day care too. But if you could work with Carrie on staying on the subject it would be helpful to all of us. Thank you.

Carrie's mom

As I read the letter, I begin to chuckle and then to laugh, finally even having to wipe away tears. This is a letter I'm going to treasure for a long, long time.

Help me, Lord, to work with Carrie and her mom in a way that will not hurt them. Help me to always focus on what is positive and to try to get to the point! Amen.

WE PUT NO STUMBLING BLOCK IN ANYONE'S PATH, SO THAT OUR MINISTRY WILL NOT BE DISCREDITED (2 CORINTHIANS 6:3).

LAURA'S STORY

*L*aura is one of my very special former students, a little girl who came to my class shy, uncertain, and withdrawn. Laura's mom says that Laura's kindergarten teacher didn't like her, but when she came to first grade she was such a talented, hard-working, and quiet little girl that it was impossible not to like her. But Laura did carry with her the damage that happened in kindergarten, and she wasn't going to take any kind of risk.

At first, she merely did her work and then sat at her desk hands primly folded. "Laura, come over here," I coaxed one day between reading groups. "I've got a great book for you to read," and I pulled out the book *Socks* by Beverly Cleary. "I'm going to read it to the class, but you could read it, too." She smiled shyly and took the book to her desk.

As I read *Socks*, Laura followed in her own book even though she was already several chapters ahead of the rest of us. When I asked the other children, "What do you think will happen next?" Laura grinned broadly—she already knew the secret!

Little by little Laura unfolded before me like a delicate flower opening on a summer day. She grew in confidence daily amid sparkles of enthusiasm.

On the playground she was no longer just an observer. With my help, she even learned to skip rope. "Laura, everyone can learn to skip rope—if I can do it, anyone can! Here I am, just a little old lady ninety years old, and here I go," I yelled as I skipped away (not too far, however). My days of skipping rope are drawing to a close.

Susan giggled in the background. "You can't be ninety, Mrs. Fisher."

Soon I was counting for Laura and watching her skip rope with light feet. With lots of encouragement, gentle good humor, and challenge, Laura finished first grade a happy little girl doing third grade tasks with great enthusiasm.

This year she's actually in third grade. I rejoice each time I see her during recess duty (and that's not prime time for me!). She always smiles and gives me a quick hug. Today I'm watching her jump rope, when all at once she seems to lose her balance, and I take off for her on the run. But she's collapsed, and by the time I get there she's unconscious. "Let's take her in," I yell to a mom who is helping out today, leaving the playground supervised by a kindergarten aide.

As we reach the office, Laura is still unconscious, but there is a good strong pulse.

Liz, the school secretary, dials 911 quickly while I sit on my knees, holding Laura's hand. I pray, "Lord, take care of this little one—she's so special and wonderful and she's your child."

Laura is awakening now, looking around with frightened eyes. "You're going to be fine, Laura," I try to reassure her.

As soon as the ambulance crew arrives, I stand back and watch, great fear assailing me. The paramedics work over her briefly, doing various medical tests. One turns to me. "She's going to be fine, we think, but we're going to take her in for observation."

Just then Laura's mother walks in and reassures Laura while helping the paramedics prepare for the trip to the hospital.

"She's such a super little girl, Lord. Be with her in these moments," I pray as I watch them load her into the ambulance.

Later I learn that Laura is fine. The diagnosis was that she probably simply jumped rope too fast without a break. She seems healthy enough when she does return to school, and I am very grateful. Sometimes a teacher's fingertips briefly brush eternity. I've had that moment with Laura.

Be with Laura, Lord. She's one of your children. Help her to know you are with her at all times, and thank you for making your presence known to all of us as you healed Laura today. Protect all children in your tender loving hands. Amen.

DO NOT BE ANXIOUS ABOUT ANYTHING, BUT IN EVERYTHING, BY PRAYER AND PETITION, WITH THANKSGIVING, PRESENT YOUR REQUESTS TO GOD. AND THE PEACE OF GOD, WHICH TRANSCENDS ALL UNDERSTANDING, WILL GUARD YOUR HEARTS AND MINDS IN CHRIST JESUS (PHILIPPIANS 4:6–7).

BUTTERFLIES IN THE MAKING

*T*he time for growing butterflies is here," I announce to my first graders one bright April morning.

I show them a jar filled with butterfly larvae. "Aren't they tiny?" I ask. "I'll pass this around so you can see them. Be very careful; they're just babies."

"Those are just green worms," huffs Jesse, but most look at the jar cautiously and then carefully pass it on.

"After school I'll put on these plastic gloves," I explain as I show them. "I'll have to be very careful and separate the larvae and put them into each little jar.

"I've already put this green nutrient in each jar. What's nutrient?" I ask.

"It's stuff to eat," Amos remembers from an earlier unit.

"Oh," they exclaim. "I wouldn't eat it," confesses Sarah.

"Well, no, of course not," I agree with her. "We wouldn't eat larvae food because we aren't larvae. Just as they wouldn't like pizza." They all laugh.

"Why can't you put them in the little jars right now?" Sarah asks.

There are thirty-two reasons.

"Tomorrow you'll each have a tiny jar for your desk," I explain.

135

The next morning as I go to bring the class in, I'm greeted with, "It's butterfly day!" They are so excited that the line has to stop twice to wait for the dancers.

In the classroom I announce the rules. "When your work is finished, you may get a larva. Each one has a name on it, so look for your own. You may take it to your desk. Can you take the lid off?"

"No," they chant.

"No," I repeat. "They're just babies; they might get sick."

All day they watch the larvae. "Look at mine, look at mine." They are proud, proud parents.

Day by day they watch the larvae eat. Finally, one day Maria yells, "Mine is making a chrysalis." Everyone gathers around to watch.

Within another couple of days, they are all chrysalides. I ask Jess, "What do you think will happen next?"

Jesse wrinkles his nose, "They could become butterflies, I guess," he admits slowly and reluctantly.

Now every morning I am greeted with, "Did the butterflies hatch?" Everyone I meet has the same question. The first grade is in the midst of a miracle, and everyone wants to know about it!

When the chrysalides formed, the children carefully removed the lids of the containers to which the chrysalides had attached. Then each tiny chrysalis still attached to the lid was transferred to an awaiting butterfly garden. Most of the children then looked at the remaining nutrient in the small jar, wrinkled their noses, and threw it away. "Don't eat it," I explain. It's always a good idea to remind first graders not to eat things like paint, glue, crayons, chalk, and butterfly nutrient!

But Joshua says, "Juan Carlos already ate his."

"Oh no, boys and girls, this is not people food," I remind them.

Juan Carlos replies, "It was good stuff; besides I didn't have any snack today."

After about ten days of watchful attention, when we come in from recess one day, Maria yells, "A butterfly has hatched! A butterfly has hatched!"

The whole class rushes to the table where we have the butterfly garden.

"Wow, look at that!" yells Andy.

Amidst cries of delight we work out a system so everyone can watch, and soon butterflies are dragging themselves out of the chrysalides, all wet and wrinkly.

Sarah comments, "We can't let them go, though; their wings have to dry."

"That's right," I praise her.

Over the next couple of days the butterflies continue to hatch. Nearly everyone in the school comes to visit. Also the butterflies visit nearly every classroom, accompanied by one or two first graders who explain the life cycle of the butterfly to other classes.

Soon our butterflies are ready to leave home. One bright, sunny afternoon we take them to the flower beds in front of the school and open the butterfly garden.

The butterflies leave one by one. "Bye, bye butterflies," my first graders wave bravely, tears in their eyes. "Bye, bye—have a good life!"

Heavenly Father, the miracles of your Creation surround us and speak eloquently of your glory. Thank you for all the beauty of the earth, but especially butterflies. Amen.

HE PERFORMS WONDERS THAT CANNOT BE FATHOMED, MIRACLES THAT CANNOT BE COUNTED (JOB 5:9).

DON'T KNOCK UNLESS THE HOUSE IS ON FIRE

I've retreated to my bedroom at home to work on a new science project for my class, but Amanda, my daughter, is also home. Every few minutes she comes in for something "really important," and then stays to talk about everything she knows. I love to visit with her, but now is not the time.

"Please, Mandy, I need to work now," I plead. "Just don't knock unless the house is on fire."

"Okay," she cheerfully assures me.

I continue to work. I haven't had such good concentration in weeks. I quickly record my thoughts as page after page flows out of my typewriter. Finally I stretch to take a break, but I smell smoke.

Quickly I touch the door. It's cool, so I open it. The air in the hallway is filled with smoke. "Amanda!" I yell. "What's burning?"

She appears at the bottom of the stairs. "Just the television," she replies. "The TV just went *phut* and it started burning," she shrugs.

"We have to get out of here!" I yell, pushing her out the front door. "Why didn't you tell me?" I ask later when the fire is out.

"You said, 'Don't knock unless the house is on fire.' It wasn't the house—it was just the TV. I'm sorry," she answers.

I hug her, grateful that we both got out of the house, but it does make me think that parents shouldn't issue too many ultimatums!

Father, thank you for our safe escape! Help me to understand that people should always be my highest priority. Thank you for Amanda and her life and help me to find more moments with her. Amen.

LET US COME BEFORE HIM WITH THANKS-GIVING (PSALM 95:2).

WE GOT THIS TERRIFIC DEAL

*A*ll the teachers are so happy about getting computers for our classrooms. There will be two computers for each room. We've all felt so out of touch with the rest of education without them.

Peggy had proudly informed us at a staff meeting, "We got this terrific deal on computers. They're secondhand but in mint condition."

Shelly had frowned and commented, "Secondhand— sometime with computers that means obsolete."

"Nonsense," Peggy had replied. "People always moan when I buy secondhand. The fact is that it's either secondhand or nothing."

When the computers arrive on brand-new tables, my class explodes with excitement. "Can we use them now?" they ask.

"I'll have to check out the software," I assure them. "So maybe tomorrow," I half promise. All throughout the day each time I glance at the computers I feel a surge of excitement.

As soon as the last little one leaves after school, I rush to the library to discover that Shelly is already there. "I'm going to check out some computer programs," I announce.

"You can have all of them," she sighs. "Not that it will do

you any good. The programs are not compatible with the computers. The computers are obsolete."

The children are still clamoring to use the computers. I try to put them off gently.

At the next teacher's meeting, Peggy says, "There are those of you who want the computers removed from your classrooms. Even though the computers are obsolete, it gives parents the idea that we're progressive just by the fact the computers are there."

"Even if they don't work?" I ask.

"Even if they don't work," she replies.

Gradually, however, the computers begin to disappear into the storage room. Finally we are told that next year the Parents' Club will be fund-raising for new computers.

Lord, thank you that your message is never obsolete. It's relevant for all ages and for all times. Help me as a teacher to not become obsolete. Help me to welcome new ideas and methods. If possible, I'd also like a computer in my classroom. Amen.

THEREFORE, IF ANYONE IS IN CHRIST, HE IS A NEW CREATION; THE OLD HAS GONE, THE NEW HAS COME! (2 CORINTHIANS 5:17).

THE RAIN FOREST

When do we get to build a rain forest?" first graders ask as early as the first day of school.

"Later, not until spring," I tell them. Every year I think that I won't do the rain forest again, because it's so much hard work. No one else turns her classroom into a rain forest; yet other children seem to learn just as well as mine. But then February rains right into the first of March. I think it's going to rain outside forever, so we may as well live in a rain forest.

We'll do a lot of discussion about rain forests and why we need them. We'll look at pictures of rain forests and maybe even see a movie. Before we start building, we'll write stories and paint pictures of rain forests. We'll know lots of things about rain forests so that we'll never be people who run around and yell, "Save the rain forests," without knowing what the rain forests are.

Our next step will be to actually build the rain forest. Ours will be a rain forest in Southeast Asia because we have so many Southeast Asian children in our town. We'll also do some cultural study after we're living in the rain forest.

First, Jim and I construct a net of yarn like a canopy near the ceiling. You don't have to have a husband to construct a rain forest, but you do have to have a very good friend!

Then the first graders start. Every day we work on leaves,

plants, flowers, and vines. We make animals and insects that live in our rain forest. A tape of a tropical thunderstorm plays in the background as we work. Joshua says, "This is the best rain forest yet."

I nod in agreement.

"We still need more flowers," Sarah prods as she finishes a bright-pink bloom.

"Careful, Mrs. Fisher, you could get wet," Maria warns as the thunderstorm hits a crescendo.

As we finish our rain forest, we are besieged by older children who come in with soft remembrance lighting their faces. "Oh, I loved living in a rain forest," they'll say, and I know it's worth it. It's the next best thing to going there!

Lord, thank you for all your living things. Instill in us the desire to care for the world you created—after all you left us in charge! Bring us joy in every creation like that joy we have experienced in our rain forest. And help me not to be too tired to do it next year! Amen.

"THE EARTH IS THE LORD'S, AND EVERYTHING IN IT" (1 CORINTHIANS 10:26).

HAPPY BIRTHDAY, DEAR TEACHER

*I*t's my birthday. Shelly has just been in my classroom to give me a Scottish plaid scarf, leather gloves for playground duty, and a chocolate eclair. Since I had no time for breakfast, I nibble the chocolate eclair, treasuring the taste of chocolate. I do love chocolate!

During recess, in the teacher's lounge there's a chocolate birthday cake from Maggie. She cuts me a piece that could come close to feeding my entire first-grade class. Valiantly I begin to eat. After all, I do love chocolate!

At lunchtime Jim comes by with flowers, the latest bestselling mystery, a croissant sandwich, and a chocolate eclair. (I manage to put that eclair in the staff refrigerator for another day.)

After lunch I begin to hear some whispers and giggles. All at once I realize that a "surprise" birthday party is in the offing. Sure enough, Adam's mom and Maria's mom come in carrying a huge chocolate sheet cake. Small voices yell, "Surprise!" and "Happy birthday!" I cut the cake in very generous pieces and think that maybe no one will notice that I don't have a piece.

"Oh, you didn't get a piece yourself," says Maria's mom, smiling as she cuts me a very large piece. "It's my family's favorite—you have to try it."

How could I refuse? It is delicious, but after a bite I slide it carefully under some papers on my desk.

As I usher the last of my class out after school, Susie, a second-grader who was in my classroom last year, peeks around the corner into my room.

"Mrs. Fisher," she grins. "My mom brought you a chocolate sundae from Baskin-Robbins!" Indeed it is not only chocolate but overloaded with whipped cream, nuts, and several maraschino cherries. I notice that there is a small sundae for Susie. I'd like to trade, but I don't want to hurt her feelings.

"She wanted to share part of your birthday with you," Susie's mom explains. "We know that you love Baskin-Robbins."

Susie eats ice cream and talks nonstop about second grade.

I try shoving ice cream around the dish, willing it to disappear.

Finally at home, I unlock the door and, as I open the door, the smell of chocolate permeates the air.

My daughter, Tricia, appears. "Hi, Mom, I'm baking you a chocolate cake!"

I try not to shudder. I'm beginning to feel like Willie Wonka, but I'm also feeling loved, and it's that feeling that prevails. As long as everyone is celebrating my birthday, I might as well sit back and enjoy it! It's great to be loved!

Our Father, thank you for all the people who helped me celebrate my birthday today! Thank you for all the wonders of the world, including chocolate, of course. A little chocolate is one of life's small joys! Amen.

SO I COMMEND THE ENJOYMENT OF LIFE, BECAUSE NOTHING IS BETTER FOR A MAN UNDER THE SUN THAN TO EAT AND DRINK AND BE GLAD. THEN JOY WILL ACCOMPANY HIM IN HIS WORK ALL THE DAYS OF THE LIFE GOD HAS GIVEN HIM UNDER THE SUN (ECCLESIASTES 8:15).

FLOWERS ... I GET FLOWERS

*I*t's a sun-kissed spring morning. On my way to get my class on the playground I hear the low, peaceful sound of a mourning dove. As I approach the line, I notice that Betsy, Maria, and Annie are standing in line, arms filled with beautiful multi-colored tulips. Within seconds after my arrival I am laden with the bouquets. "I love tulips," I tell them. "They're so beautiful. Thank you very much."

Back in the classroom, it takes almost every container I've collected over the years to accommodate all the tulips. Yesterday we did a tulip art project, so the room looks like a festive garden.

We are all working very industriously when Peggy comes into the room. "Your room looks wonderful," she comments. "Where did you get the tulips?"

"Oh, Betsy, Maria, and Annie brought them," I smile.

"Did you know that the school's tulips that I planted by the office last fall are gone? Every single one of them. These tulips, in fact, look very much like them!"

I look over at Betsy, Maria, and Annie. Their faces are pink flushed and Maria's little body is shivering even though it's very warm in the room.

"I think I'd better see them in the office," asserts Peggy. By this time there are big bursts of sobs coming from all three girls as they reluctantly follow Peggy out of the room.

It was after recess when my young outlaws returned to the room.

Maria runs to me, her arms outstretched. "We didn't know we weren't supposed to pick them. We wanted to give you flowers!"

"Thank you," I hug her, also including my other two villains in my arms. "You just have to remember that something has to belong to you before you can give it to someone else."

Still the tulips ARE beautiful.

Dear Lord, help me to lead these children on the path of righteousness and truth. Help me to correct them with tenderness and loving concern when they stray from that path. Help me not to lose that path either! Amen.

EVEN A CHILD IS KNOWN BY HIS ACTIONS, BY WHETHER HIS CONDUCT IS PURE AND RIGHT (PROVERBS 20:11).

DEAR FIRST GRADERS

*I*t's the last day of school. All the awards for the year have been given, all the Pledges of Allegiances have been said, and all the "God, Bless America"'s have been sung. All the desks have been cleaned, all the chalkboards have been erased. My desk is stacked high with gifts, flowers, and cards. It's time to say good-bye.

I pass out copies of the letter I've written to them. "We'll read it together," I suggest. They nod comfortably, for at some time this year they began to read. They've opened a door that has changed their lives forever. Soon now they'll walk through that door and into the hallway of life. They'll never be first graders again.

We begin to read in unison:

Dear First Graders,

We've had such a wonderful year together. Remember all the exciting things we did? Remember the cakewalk when we gave all those luscious cakes away? Remember how we lived in a rain forest? Remember the butterflies? Remember the time we went on a secret mission and found spring? Remember Rollerworld? Remember our secret word? Remember all the books we read? Remember all the fun we had?

I watch small fingers carefully underlining each word as we read it, not too fast so that Joshua, Max, and Juan Carlos can keep up. I watch small faces glow and the smiles of remembrance. We go on;

> There are so many things I wish for you.
> I wish you sunshine.
> I wish you umbrellas when it rains.
> I wish you flowers, and birds singing, and butterflies waving.
> I wish you toasty warm toes in the winter.
> I wish you pizza with extra cheese.
> I wish you beanbags and books.
> I wish you smiles and giggles.
> I wish you rainbows.
> I wish you love.
> Be happy my wonderful first graders. Be happy, super-stars!
>
> Love,
>
> Mrs. Fisher

As we conclude, I can no longer hold back my tears and neither can they. "Anyway, they're tears of happiness," says Maria as the tiny drops roll down her cheeks and drip off her chin.

It's time for the last tearful hugs and last good-byes. As I watch them leave for the very last time, I pick up a note from my desk. "I wish you so many wonderfuls you can't count them. Love, Adam."

I have them already, Adam. Tears falling freely, I pick up another note. It says, "Dere Fisher, Love, Max." Dear, dear Max and dear, dear first graders!

Heavenly Father, bless and keep all first graders, all little ones and the bigger ones who teach them! Thank you for all the joys of teaching! Amen.

BE JOYFUL ALWAYS; PRAY CONTINUALLY; GIVE THANKS IN ALL CIRCUMSTANCES, FOR THIS IS GOD'S WILL FOR YOU IN CHRIST JESUS (1 THESSALONIANS 5:16).